HUGH PALMER *The Most*

Thames & Hudson

Beautiful Villages of Normandy

WITH 256 ILLUSTRATIONS IN COLOR

Half-title page
The traditional half-timbered buildings of the Auberge du Vieux Puits at Pont-Audemer (Eure).

Title pages
Regnéville-sur-Mer (Manche) from the south.

Opposite
The architectural ages of the Normandy village (left to right): *half-timbering at Ry (Seine-Maritime); 'Normanesque' at Houlgate (Calvados); medieval on Mont-Saint-Michel (Manche); 'Promenade' at Étretat (Seine-Maritime).*

Acknowledgments

Thanks is due to all the representatives of the departmental and regional tourist authorities who met my requests for help and information with their customary efficiency and friendliness. I am especially grateful to Jane Rickard and Stephen Rodgers at the Normandy Tourist Board's Bristol office for making all the necessary introductions to their colleagues in France.

I owe a great debt of gratitude to my wife Hoonie, who has put up with the absentee lifestyle of a photographer in the past and now has to contend with the anti-social habits of an author when I am at home. She is also a wonderful travelling companion, and in anticipation of many trips together in the future, I dedicate this book to her, with love.

H.P.

© 2002 Thames & Hudson Ltd, London
Text & photographs © 2002 Hugh Palmer

First published in hardcover in the United States of America in 2002 by Thames & Hudson Inc., 500 Fifth Avenue, New York, New York 10110

thamesandhudsonusa.com

Library of Congress Catalog Card Number 2001093461
ISBN 0-500-51072-5

Printed and bound in Singapore by C. S. Graphics

Contents

Introduction

THE LANDSCAPE OF NORMANDY is full of rich and diverse treats. Divided into five *départements*, the region encompasses the sandy beaches of the Côte Fleurie, the rocky crags of the Suisse Normande, profusely wooded valleys inland, and the ancient forests round which the great river Seine curls and meanders on its way to its huge estuary beside the port of Le Havre.

In fact, Normandy is not one but two distinct geographical regions. The western half, known as Basse-Normandie, is characterized by the irregular shapes of its eroded rocky landscape – the granite-based Armorican Massif which it shares with its rugged neighbour to the west, Brittany. Haute-Normandie, occupying the eastern half of the region, is typically flatter, a wide-spreading plateau of sedimentary limestone, bounded spectacularly by the coast between Le Havre and Dieppe – the famous Côte d'Albâtre, with its gleaming, towering white cliffs.

These two regions were first bound together as a political entity by another unstoppable force – the military might of the Normans. In 911 the Frankish king Charles the Simple ceded the region to Rollo, leader of a band of Danish Vikings, thus making him the first Duke of Normandy. In preceding centuries, this rich land had become one of the destinations of choice for the pillaging expeditions of the Vikings. Charles (called 'the Simple' for his straightforwardness rather than his dimness) calculated that Rollo and his men would consolidate the defences of the Île de France against further invasions along the Seine. This they did, turning their own invading skills northward towards England only one hundred and fifty years later under the celebrated leadership of Duke William, bastard son of Rollo's great-great-grandson Robert the Magnificent. William's own wrangling offspring would be involved, variously, in alliances and warfare with the Frankish kings in the years that followed, but inter-marriage and a mingling of the two

*T*he former eminence of Honfleur (Calvados) as a trading port is reflected in the grand houses and shops which line the Quai Sainte-Catherine, viewed here across the Vieux Bassin.

7

Traditional building in Normandy: one of eleven surviving twelfth-century towers looms over a half-timbered house in Domfront (Orne) (top); a traditional flint and brick wall lines part of the main street in Giverny (Eure) (above).

cultures eventually blurred distinctions between the French and Norman way of life.

The strong influence of the early Normans appears everywhere in the dukedom. Their seafaring forays built up the prosperity of the coastal ports, from which explorers set out to find new lands to conquer. By the twelfth century, Norman territories included the kingdom of Sicily and parts of southern Italy, eventually stretching as far as Mesopotamia. Later still, it was to be the Normans who began the colonization of eastern Canada.

The visitor to Normandy will also be impressed by the architectural legacy of the dukes. They converted readily to Christianity and demonstrated their enthusiasm for the new religion by the foundation of countless monasteries and cathedrals, many built in the style that bears their name. Fortresses, too, were constructed in great numbers; in the southern border country, the threat of attack by the French persuaded the Conqueror's descendants to fortify as many strongholds as possible.

In keeping with the warlike character of the region's first rulers, it is no surprise to find that many of Normandy's ancient villages huddle around a hilltop château. This was the safest way to guard against attack from outside; it also reflected the sophisticated system of feudal government developed by the Norman nobility under which the productive resources of the peasants, in return for armed protection, supported the war-lords who in turn owed their fealty to the duke. In some cases, the château has disappeared: at Lyons-la-Forêt, for instance, where a ring of stone houses (built from the castle remains) surrounds a circular mound where the castle once stood. At Domfront in Orne, the entire village is defensively sited along the crest of a lofty rocky outcrop. The castle, at the western end of the ridge, was the preferred base of King Henry I, who held court there when he was in Normandy.

The palatial pretensions of the seaside 'Normanesque' style (right) are seen to full advantage on the Avenue des Alliés in Houlgate (Calvados).

Grandeur of another age: the château of Vauville (Manche) was begun at the end of the 16th century and finished at the beginning of the 17th.

Other settlements have strong religious associations: Sées, with its magical twin-towered cathedral, owes its importance to a bishopric that dates from the year 400. Of equal antiquity, and with its extraordinary position combining the sacred with the militarily strategic, famous Mont-Saint-Michel stands like a watchful sentinel off the Manche coast. It has been threatened countless times during its long history, but it has never been overrun, except by the armies of visitors who now flock to it all the year round. Such survivals, unfortunately, are the exception rather than the rule; many buildings from the Norman period and before had survived until the twentieth century, only to be destroyed during the fierce fighting which followed the Allied landings of 1944.

The coastline, so distinctive from, and yet so close to the orchard-rich countryside inland, has its own diverse range of villages. Removed from the somewhat pretentious grandeur of the Norman Riviera, whose resorts became fashionable during the Second Empire, such seaside gems as Houlgate and Étretat have a more home-spun air; the architectural fantasies of their 'Normanesque' villas can be admired during a stroll along their tree-lined avenues. Further along the coast, Port-en-Bessin and Barfleur are coastal settlements whose history reaches back far further than the imagination of a mid-nineteenth-century entrepreneur. Both are fishing ports of great antiquity; Barfleur, especially, sheltered by the Cotentin peninsula on whose eastern coast it lies, benefited from its proximity to England to become the royal embarkation point for successive Norman monarchs and their courts.

*T*he sixteenth-century reconstruction of the twelfth-century church of Sainte-Radégonde (above) *in Giverny (Eure) sits squatly in its churchyard, the burial place of Claude Monet.*

*O*utside the Halles of Dives-sur-Mer (Calvados) (above right) *traditional half-timbered construction conceals further glories of woodwork within.*

*T*he hillside location of Mortain (Manche) in the valley of the Cance makes for dramatic effects of rocks and water, like the Petite Cascade viewed from the Pont du Diable (opposite).

Inland, in Basse-Normandie, the rocky outcrops of the Armorican Massif are the setting for hill villages, such as Clécy and Mortain. The latter's collegiate church of Saint-Évroult looms over the village, the stark lines of its Gothic bell-tower harmonizing with the obdurate material from which it was built seven hundred years ago – granite, from which most of the village's houses also come. The character of the Mortainais is a far cry (although a mere eighty kilometres distant) from the countryside around Beuvron-en-Auge, which sits plumply in the woodland and pastures east of Caen. The half-timbered houses of its meticulously restored village centre attest to a long history of prosperity, founded on the apple orchards and pastureland of the Pays d'Auge.

Normandy's great skies are constantly refreshed by the weather blowing in from the Atlantic. The westerly winds spend much of their ferocity over Brittany; here they are reduced to the welcome role of watering the countryside to a high level of fertility, filling the skies with the rich and ever-changing cloudscapes beloved by generations of painters, both native and adopted, who have been seduced by the province's wonderfully varied countryside.

Manche

The Quai Tourville by the fishing harbour of Saint-Vaast-la-Hougue is still the site of a boat-repair yard for the local fleet. Inland the rolling wooded country of Manche reveals itself (opposite), *viewed from the ridge of Mortain towards the south.*

IT IS IMPOSSIBLE TO ESCAPE THE SEA and its influence in the *département* of Manche. Even if one retreats to the heights of its hinterland – the rocky hills of the Mortainais – a scramble to the highest peak will, on a clear day, reveal the vision, dear to the medieval pilgrim, of Mont-Saint-Michel shimmering in its bay, not fifty kilometres distant. Even an area of classic Norman pastureland, like the marshy stretch which lies between Lessay and the Baie des Veys, may look like dry land, but if the sea rose by a mere ten metres, it would be submerged and the peninsula of Cotentin become once more an island. This promontory, jutting northwards into the Channel, has a wild character and a rainfall that resemble those of neighbouring Brittany. Its main port, Cherbourg, has lost much of its passenger trade to the more accessible harbours to the east but, as a result, the villages, churches and fortified manors around remain an unspoilt delight for the inquisitive visitor.

Over on the eastern shore, Barfleur and its string of small fishing ports shelter from the westerly gales, while the west coast of the Cotentin loses its rugged, weather-beaten aspect as the coastline leads down to Granville. By the time it gets to Mont-Saint-Michel, where Normandy ends and Brittany begins, the high winds and pounding breakers have given way to the less dramatic but more powerful tidal flows which have changed the coastline and rendered a number of harbours useless through silting.

After the 1944 Allied landings, Manche experienced much of the heavy fighting that followed, despite the rapid thrust towards Paris. The Cotentin had to be freed to establish Cherbourg as a supply base, while to the south the hilly area around Mortain saw a terrible struggle as the Allies tried to dislodge the German Seventh Army. The capital of the *département*, Saint-Lô, was liberated at great cost; almost every building there was destroyed.

Barfleur

DESPITE LONG-STANDING CLAIMS to the contrary, Barfleur was not the point of embarkation for Duke William when he set sail from Normandy to conquer England. It would have been a logical choice, however, for it had been a port since before the arrival of the Vikings. But its shipyards did provide the Conqueror's vessel, the *Mora*, and it was steered by a helmsman from Barfleur – these facts are recorded on a plaque attached to a boulder by the village church of Saint-Nicolas.

Barfleur ended up greatly benefiting from William's victorious expedition; it was, after all, the closest viable port to England. Cherbourg might have been a few miles closer, but it would be many centuries before sea defences could be built to counter its exposure to the north-westerly gales. Meanwhile, around the coast, the harbour gained some shelter from the Pointe de Barfleur, although the approach was made hazardous by treacherous currents and reefs. Nevertheless, the increase in cross-Channel traffic quickly made it the busiest port in Normandy, used by all the Anglo-Norman kings for the crossing between their kingdoms. In 1120, an ill-fated royal voyage was to plunge the English court into mourning, after a ship ran foul of the Barfleur reefs and sank. This was the *White Ship* of William Atheling, son and heir of Henry I; his death, with that of his sister and 300 of his retinue, left the king a broken man for the rest of his reign.

Barfleur had its own sorrows to face, paying for its popularity with the Norman kings when Edward III sacked it in 1346. By that time it had grown to be a town of six thousand inhabitants, quite unlike the quiet harbour-village it has since become. Its main street, the Rue Saint-Thomas, is broad and stately, but the harbour to which it leads still retains the small scale of its past. Diminutive granite-built mansions line the quays, which are often piled high with lobster-pots. Such small-scale coastal fishing is now the speciality of Barfleur's fishermen, but pride in their port is evident as they assure their quayside customers that the lobsters of Barfleur are the finest on the coast.

*B*arfleur's sturdy-looking church stands at the head of the quay in the fishing harbour; its spire was removed in 1767, being judged unstable in high winds.

*T*he solid-looking house façades along the main quay and in the Rue du Fort of Barfleur hint at the little port's prosperity through the centuries (this page); this wealth, created through maritime effort, is wonderfully symbolized by the upstream light against the sky (opposite).

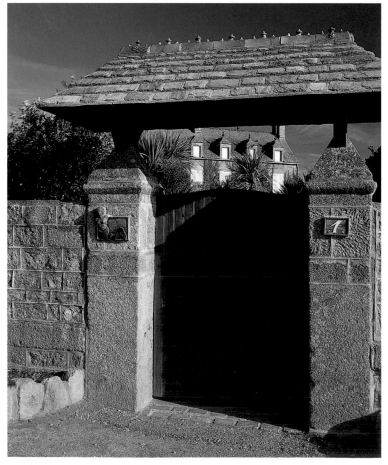

Mont-Saint-Michel

THERE ARE A FEW MAN-MADE MARVELS whose
first sighting effortlessly eclipses their description
and visual representation; but Mont-Saint-Michel
can be reliably numbered among them. The flatness
of its surroundings makes such a vertical
exclamation point the more striking. This 'gigantic
granite jewel', as Guy de Maupassant called it, is the
extraordinary result of eight centuries of
architectural accretion, reflecting the demands of
church and nation for successive rebuilding to
increase both the spiritual and the defensive
authority of the mount.

Ever since the river Couesnon, which flows into
the Baie Saint-Michel, became the boundary
between the dukedoms of Brittany and Normandy,
the impregnability of the mount made it a decisive
stronghold. No less than three robust gatehouses
must be passed before visitors can make their way
up the main street which climbs steeply towards the
citadel. The souvenir stalls which line this narrow
thoroughfare would not, in their appearance or in
their exorbitant prices, have seemed unfamiliar to
the pious thousands who have made their hazardous
pilgrimage here since the Middle Ages.

Long after the monastic community had
shrivelled to a mere handful of monks, the post-
Revolutionary government finally stripped the
mount of its religious status, turning it into a gaol; it
housed many distinguished political prisoners,
before public outcry (in which the enthusiastic and
weighty voice of Victor Hugo was heard) persuaded
the government to commence restoration. A
causeway was built in 1877, and the tide of tourists,
the pilgrims of our secular age, continues to flow
there by the dozens of coach-loads. It will be
interesting to see what happens if present plans to
remove the causeway (to counter the silting-up of
the bay) are carried out, and this celestial place
becomes once again an island.

*Viewed from the Porte du Roi, the Gothic towers and battlements of
the mount loom over more modest dwellings (above). At dawn,
seen from the flood plains which surround it, Mont-Saint-Michel thrusts
a mighty ecclesiastical and military presence skywards (opposite).*

These pages

The sense of peace and tranquillity which permeates the inner court of the cloisters on a high point of the mount belies their improbably precarious position above the tumult of the ocean below.

Overleaf

The military and the religious are inseparably entwined in the architecture of the mount which presents itself in concentric fashion. First, there are outer defences, punctuated by severe-looking flights of steps, followed by more distinctly domestic dwellings (p.23), and capped by what is effectively an ecclesiastical fortress of formidable presence.

Mortain

The rocky valley of the Cance and the high granite crags that surround Mortain could easily have earned the region the name of 'Suisse Normande', had not the almost as dramatic Cléçois, over in Calvados, been thus termed first. Certainly, the picturesque waterfalls, reached by a wooded path from the village, caught the eye of several nineteenth-century painters, including Courbet, who returned there several times around 1850. Earlier pilgrims climbed to the top of the Rocher Brûlé, as is evidenced by the small chapel perched on the summit; from there, on an extremely clear day, they could see their eventual destination, Mont-Saint-Michel, which must have looked to them like a vision of the celestial city itself. A surer bet on most days is an extended view towards Maine in the south and a bird's-eye view of the village below.

The apparent severity of the collegiate church of Saint-Évroult and its bell-tower, its starkly vertical lines accentuated by the tallest of lancet windows, should not deter the visitor. The interior of the church, entered through a cheerful south portal (whose style can be fairly described as Flamboyant Norman), is surprisingly welcoming - its character, as André Bazin observed, 'pious and tender'. The choir has some of the finest carved stalls in Normandy, the fifteenth-century misericords showing, among other figures, the patron saints of shoe-making, Saint Crespin and Saint Crespinien, at their lasts. In any case, the church has good reason to present its hard granite exterior proudly to the world: its capacity for survival was put to the sternest test during the battles of August 1944, as American forces, with great difficulty and huge casualties, dislodged the defending German Seventh Army. Eighty per cent of the village was reduced to ruins; the church, and the nearby Abbaye Blanche, however, miraculously escaped destruction.

Seen from the west, the village stretches out along granite crags and escarpments in the wooded valley of the Cance. The bell-tower of Saint-Évroult dominates the rooftops clustered around it.

*T**he riverside and distinctly rocky location of Mortain makes for*
steep streets and sturdy stone buildings (above). The chapel of
Saint- Michel (1852), on the site of an old oratory (above right), marks
the highest point of the village ridge. Below, near the Place du Château,
the houses seem a natural continuation of the local granite (right).

*M*ortain's collegiate church of Saint-Évroult is a veritable treasure-house of architectural and decorative delights: a doorway in the Flamboyant Norman style (right); fifteenth-century carved misericords in the choir (below); and an extraordinary seventh-century Irish chrismal (below right).

*N*ow a haven of retreat, the twelfth-century Abbaye Blanche is
a piece of engagingly simple, sturdy building. The barrel vaulting
of its cellars (above) rises from plainly decorated capitals; the cloisters
(substantially restored) adjoin the long sisters' refectory.

Regnéville-sur-Mer

*I*n spite of the silting-up of Regnéville's port, a common phenomenon on the coast of the Cotentin, this boatyard (below) still functions to service pleasure craft. This church (opposite), the oldest of three in the village, dates from the twelfth century, making it roughly as old as the ruins of the adjoining donjon.

THE WEST COAST of the Cotentin peninsula, as it faces the Atlantic, has quite a repertoire of different characters. Towards its northern tip, exposure to wild seas has given it a rugged coastline, with windswept cliffs and rock-girt inlets – about as Breton as Normandy ever gets. But by the time the roads south have reached the area around Coutances, the pastures inland are flatter, the sea milder and the coast more relaxed. A stretch of fine sand has enabled Coutainville to become a bathing resort, albeit a rather sleepy one, while just to the south, the river Sienne snakes into the sea with not much more than a sand bar to shelter its estuary. Surprisingly, however, the tiny village of Regnéville-sur-Mer was once a busy port.

An enjoyable stroll past its neat parade of seaside villas, now looking out over dunes, will quickly turn up clues to this prosperous past. First, there are the remains of a substantial castle, dating from the twelfth century and important enough to have had its destruction ordered by Richelieu himself. Past the church and up the hill, there is a museum devoted to the activities of the area, including the coastal specialities of boat-building, rope-making and kelp-picking. An interesting reconstruction in an adjacent quarry explains the big secret of the port's success: lime-kilns, active until the end of the last century, busy turning the local *calcaire* into lime, which was then shipped out of Regnéville for the Channel Islands and Brittany. Also used as a basis for primitive fertilizers, lime was the vital ingredient in the mortar used for building work, until the industrialized production of cement became widespread in the 1880s. After that, all this industry quickly dwindled and there were soon too few ships visiting the port for serious inconvenience to be caused by the steady silting that eventually separated Regnéville from the sea.

*O*nce in the hands of the family of the Conqueror, the village donjon (opposite) *must have been a formidable building when intact. Present-day Regnéville, though, is essentially a place of pleasant villas and houses.*

Saint-Vaast-la-Hougue

*B*oth fishing port and marina
(opposite), the village was
fortified by Vauban in the 17th
century; its Chapelle des Marins
(above) traditionally acted as a
landmark for fishing vessels.

SAINT-VAAST manages a similar feat to that achieved by Cancale in Brittany: to be a north-coast port and yet at the same time to have a harbour that faces virtually due south. Perhaps because of their uniquely sheltered positions, both ports share another claim to fame - the deliciousness of the oysters raised on their mudflats. But Saint-Vaast's maritime history goes back further than its present harbour, which a busy fishing fleet now shares with a marina: Edward III landed here on his way to start the Hundred Years War, and just by the harbour entrance is a Romanesque votary chapel.

In 1694, that seemingly ubiquitous fortifier-in-waiting to Louis XIV, Sébastien le Prestre de Vauban, arrived here. He had an urgent brief: two years before, the forty-four ships of Louis' admiral, the Comte de Tourville, were cornered off Saint-

Vaast by an allied fleet of ninety English and Dutch men-of-war. The French flotilla, which had been ordered by Louis to attempt an invasion of England, held out for a whole day, but then, without a protective harbour, suffered heavy losses from fire-ships. Vauban's solution was to defend the harbour entrance from both sides: he built two circular cannon-towers, one at the end of La Hougue, the sandy spit running south from the harbour, the other on the nearby island of Tatihou, with an additional garrison fort on the adjoining islet. The fort, the tower and other relics of Tatihou's varied roles – quarantine zone, children's home and now nature reserve – can be inspected by taking an amphibious ferry from Saint-Vaast or, at low tide, walking across the mudflats on a causeway that leads past the oyster beds.

Vauville

THE WIND-BUFFETED WALKER on the barren cliff-tops of the Nez de Jobourg, highest and most westerly point of the Cotentin peninsula, can descend with gratitude to the quieter coastline to the south. Here, looking out over a wide bay, Vauville sits sheltered in a setting of bracken and heather. A steep-sided valley brings fresh water into a small lagoon, formerly the property of the priory, which stands on a hill above the village. A Richard de Vauville, grandson of Guillaume of that name, was responsible for founding this priory, dedicated to St. Michael, in 1147. He also built the first castle to stand in the village, a mighty defensive affair which had fallen into ruin by the time a replacement was built on the same site, incorporating the only part to survive from the earlier edifice – a tower complete with its spiral staircase.

Stone-faced cottages line the main street of the village, under which runs the picturesque local brook (these pages).

This newer castle, finished in the early seventeenth century, has a Scottish air about it, which blends with the heather. The garden of the château itself, however, holds a pleasant geographical surprise: it is full of rare and tender plants, many of them collected from the southern hemisphere. This botanical labour of love has been the work of Eric and Nicole Pellerin, whose parents took the property over after it had been sadly damaged during the Second World War. For those whose taste for the rugged draws them away from the peaceful business of garden visiting, Vauville makes the best of its position to offer wind-powered entertainment, including gliding at the famous field of Maneyrol, hang-gliding from the ancient sacrificial site of Pierre-Pouquelée, and even wind-powered charioteering on the long beach of the Anse de Vauville.

*S*imple yet authoritative, the twelfth-century church of Saint-Martin stands discreetly behind the village château (opposite); *a few more decorative elements embellish the equally straightforward interior (*right *and* below).

There is something specially moving about the combination of rugged stone building and running water which makes Vauville's main street a particularly pleasing arrangement.

*S*ecular and snug the houses of Vauville's main street may be (left), but the religious affiliations of the place are all around. A cross crowns the windswept downland in-shore of the village (above). On another hill lies the priory of Saint-Martin, seen here from a position close to the church of the same name (opposite).

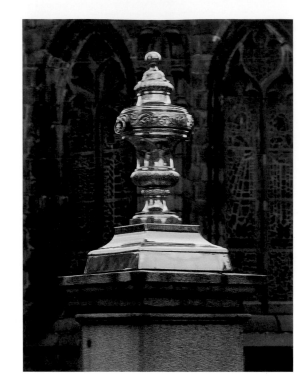

Fittingly, in a town famed for its production of cooking pans, the ornament which adorns the top of a plinth (right) in the Place de la République is of copper. Close by runs the Rue du Docteur Harvard (below and opposite), a peaceful relief from the bustle of the main square.

Villedieu-les-Poêles

BREASTING A RISE TO THE NORTH, the road from Caen gives a fine view of Villedieu, before it runs down towards the long, sloping market square and the grand bell-tower of the church of Notre-Dame. The first community to settle in the loop made here by the river Sienne was known as Siennêtre, a modest trading settlement within reach of the rich farmland of the southern bocage. A turn in the place's fortunes came during Henry Beauclerck's reign, when he gave some nearby land to the Order of the Hospitallers of St. John of Jerusalem. They founded one of their first commanderies here, and later changed the village's name to Villedieu.

By that time, a thriving trade had grown up in pots and pans hammered out of copper and tin. The craft of the *poesliers* (*poêle* meaning frying-pan) had been developed since the twelfth century – by the middle of the eighteenth, there were several hundred workshops, many clustered along the river Sienne, from whose power they fired their furnaces. Another specialist craft, the casting of bells, also made Villedieu's name famous. Happily, one of the original bell-foundries is still in operation, although only a very fortunately timed visit will coincide with the rare and dramatic pouring of molten bronze to fill the huge moulds. The techniques, unchanged since the Middle Ages, are still demonstrated, including the mixing of the traditional material from which the giant moulds are formed – a tough, pliable and very smelly mix of clay, goat's hair and horse-dung.

Serious-looking saucepans are for sale in the numerous gift-shops, together with every knick-knack that can possibly be fashioned from copper. The real treasures to be discovered, however, are the tiny medieval courtyards leading off the older streets, some the site of ancient workshops, as suggested by their names: Cour de l'Enfer, Cour du Foyer, for instance. The survival of these rarities is proof of Villedieu's continuing good fortune: it escaped completely unscathed from the destruction of 1944.

*M*any of the traditional workshops of Villedieu have survived, along with the traditional crafts of tin and copper beating (opposite *and* above). *One bell foundry* (left) *has been in continuous operation since medieval times. Decorative moulds in a local shop* (left above) *display the extent of the copper-beater's art.*

*T*he strange square tower of the church of Notre-Dame (above)
towers over the neat little streets and buildings (including a
handsome Mairie) of Villedieu (right above *and* left). *Fascinating
and slightly mysterious courtyards, often the setting of former copper
workshops* (opposite), *lead off from the principal streets.*

THE VIKING SEA-RAIDERS who were effectively the first Normans never turned their backs on the sea, even after they had become successful settlers on mainland France. At first, it was the river Seine which provided access from the sea for their trading and pillaging expeditions, and for the influx of settlers who came to join them from Scandinavia. After they had achieved control of the whole of Normandy, they secured harbours along the coastline.

In Dieppe (a name derived from the Norse word for 'deep') they found a port already developed by earlier Saxon invaders. In the sixteenth century this became the home of an extensive fleet of privateers, assembled by Dieppe's most famous mariner, Jean Ango. It also became the first bathing resort, after members of the court of Napoleon III took up the new fashion. Then followed the rapid establishment of numerous resorts along the Normandy coast; the Côte Fleurie, the stretch of sandy beaches west of Honfleur, boasts the most prestigious among these, the names of Deauville and Trouville resonant with the elegance of the Parisian upper classes who flocked to them annually. Older ports along this part of the coast, such as Dives-sur-Mer, have seen their harbours pushed back from the sea by the accumulation of silt from the mouth of the Seine; it was from there that Duke William set off to conquer England. Almost nine hundred years later an invasion force coming in the opposite direction fought its way on to the Normandy beaches to begin the painful process of France's liberation.

Ports and Harbours

*T*he beaches of Normandy bear the scars of conflict and decline: a World War II block-house stands at the edge of Omaha Beach (opposite), with the Pointe du Hoc in the background. Below the cliffs near Varengeville-sur-Mer, a former landing stage seems to be disappearing back into the pebbled beach (below).

*T*he history of the Normandy coast is coloured by naval and land engagements and by the development of the fishing industry; at Port-en-Bessin (Calvados) a seventeenth-century defensive tower by Vauban looks towards the fish-market on the quay (opposite). Modern maritime activity, though, is just as likely to be concerned with pleasure: the new marina at Dives-sur-Mer (Calvados).

*C*liffs, beaches, stony harbours – the Normandy coast has them all: the Manneporte from the Falaise d'Aval at Étretat (Seine-Maritime) (opposite); a deserted beach west of Varengeville-sur-Mer (Seine-Maritime), towards Sainte-Marguerite (above); the harbour mouth (left) at Saint-Vaast-la-Hougue (Manche).

Calvados

*T*he war and peace of Normandy: at Crépon a memorial (above) to the men of the Royal Greenjackets, sculpted by Jim Butler, marks the furthest point forward reached by any unit on the first day of the D-Day landings; in present-day Normandy, Clécy seems entirely at peace in its valley (opposite).

LIKE ITS FAMOUS APPLE BRANDY, the *département* of Calvados is a rich distillation. It lies at the centre of Normandy and has in profusion those elements that have always attracted the visitor to the province: a string of beach resorts along its coast and the most verdant and fruitful countryside inland. 'Rich' is certainly a word that applies to the coast that leads from jewel-like Honfleur towards Caen – the Côte Fleurie, where the smart resorts of Deauville and Trouville have been in vogue since the nineteenth century.

To the south, the Pays d'Auge is an agricultural landscape of the utmost charm. The productivity of its lush orchards and pastures has meant the preservation of many of its traditional farming ways and of its half-timbered manor-houses. Lisieux in the heart of this country has its local saint Thérèse to honour; Falaise to the west is grateful for the less spiritual virtues of its eleventh-century Arlette, a tanner's daughter whose beauty captivated the younger son of Robert II, Duke of Normandy. The product of their liaison turned out to be the most famous of the ducal line, William the Bastard, later to become William the Conqueror. On the far side of the craggy region known as the 'Suisse Normande', the countryside of Calvados becomes once more a tapestry of rolling green, divided by banked-up hedgerows. Marshier and sparser, the Bessin region was the scene of some of the fiercest fighting after the huge Allied invasion of June 1944. It was along the coast of the Bessin, and further along the Côte de Nacre towards Caen, that the armada of 132,000 men landed on the beaches – the largest invasion force in history, and the first of any size to land in Normandy since Henry V arrived in 1415.

Beuvron-en-Auge

RICH FARMLAND, half-timbered manor-houses, and a cornucopia of delicious produce – several of the key elements of everyone's dreams about Normandy seem to be concentrated in the Pays d'Auge. The fertility of the pastureland here, increased for centuries by the deliberate flooding of vast water-meadows by the river has always created easy wealth for the farmer, and there are plenty of indications of a leisured lifestyle. It is in this region that the rustic style of building with timber reached its flamboyant peak, with every showy architectural fashion duly added to the manorial farmhouse or outbuildings. Even the sublime crafts of the *cidrier* and *fromagiste* are an indication that life has not been that hard – surely farmers who had a struggle to subsist on ungrateful land would not have had the energy to direct to sidelines usually left to the womenfolk?

Into such a setting of luxuriance, picture-book Beuvron fits perfectly. Both in and around the village, there were already original buildings surviving from the 15th century onwards – wonderfully timbered manors, inns, farms – when an enterprising mayor decided at the beginning of the 1970s that the ensemble would make an outstanding tourist attraction. Skilful restoration has made the oval-shaped main market-place a feast of architectural treasures. At its centre is the elegant covered market. In October, a cider festival is held here, but all year round it is difficult to resist the many roadside signs that tempt the visitor to turn off down some grassy track to sample the sublime beverage of the region, refined over the centuries.

The village is remarkable for its wealth of traditional Norman half-timbered building (above *and* opposite), *much of which has been lovingly restored in recent decades.*

*A*round the main street and central square of the
village (these pages) cluster the typically Norman
houses which have made Beuvron such an attraction
for visitors from all over the province.

Capital of the Suisse Normande, Clécy has a fine church with a late medieval belfry (above) and an interior restored in the 19th century (right). Secular power is represented by an unassuming Mairie (opposite).

Clécy

WHETHER OR NOT the area of winding roads, crags and rushing rivers deserves a title quite as grandiose as 'Suisse Normande', Clécy's claim to be called its capital is not to be challenged. It sits high on a rocky plateau, many of its older houses built from the local granite and schist, and has a hill-village air if not quite an Alpine one. The river Orne sweeps by below in one of its less turbulent moods, past old mill-houses, weeping willows and recreational facilities. Further downstream it cuts deeply through the limestone and careers down through deep canyons, where brightly clad canoeists bob about like corks on the water, while rock-climbers dangle from ropes and hang-gliders soar from the crags that tower above the curving course of the river and the woods which line it.

These animated scenes and the general touristic popularity of the area must be welcome sights to older residents, who can remember not only a hard living on the difficult terrain, but also dreadful months of bitter fighting and destruction as the Allied forces pushed slowly and painfully through the area in 1944. Thury-Harcourt to the north ('gateway to the Suisse Normande') lost its beautiful château, and with it unfortunately the wonderful works of art and furnishings assembled by its owner, François-Henri, Duc d'Harcourt, in the 18th century. The duke was also a passionate gardener and writer on horticultural matters. His charming garden layout has survived, sloping down towards the banks of the Orne. On a fine evening, the garden manages to give the castle the allure of a romantic ruin.

Dives-sur-Mer

*F*açades of various ages and styles enliven the streets of Dives (above). *Behind that of the Hostellerie Guillaume le Conquérant, off the Rue d'Hastings, is a lively craft market (opposite).*

THE NAME 'Dives-sur-Mer' at first strikes the visitor as being as spurious as the sign which pronounces this to be the 'village de Guillaume le Conquérant' at the entrance to its touristic craft centre. For 'Dives', as it is more realistically known in the locality, is now a good kilometre from the sea after its river access silted up centuries ago. In fact, the village did gain its early prosperity from its fishing fleet, and Duke William did set sail for England from here in 1066. Seven thousand troops were billeted here through that summer, as unfavourable weather delayed the invasion plans for England, and a huge depot of martial equipment was described as being piled up on the beach.

Sudden and dramatic tides of good fortune were not unknown to Dives: fifty-five years before the invasion of England, one of its fishing craft had turned up a figure of the crucified Christ in its nets. This was installed in a small chapel in the village, and by William's time was already attracting a flow of pilgrims. Whether or not he chose Dives as his setting-out point because of this holy connection is not known, but on his return as victor the following year he endowed the local abbey with funds to build a church to house the reliquary.

Not much of the original structure is visible in the present church of Notre-Dame, though its huge size gives a hint of its past importance. Equally grand and almost as lofty is the timber-covered market a couple of streets away. A good deal of its massive framing has stood, reinforced by iron bands, since the sixteenth century. On Saturday mornings a market is held, and the Halles is filled with food and craft stalls and a press of shoppers – such a crowd that the market overflows into the adjoining main square and the narrow streets around. Many of the prosperous-looking clientele come from Dives' new yacht marina, Port Guillaume, and its trendy ziggurat of desirable apartment buildings, ready proof that Dives is once again 'sur-Mer'.

The interior of the Halles (left) was entirely rebuilt after the Second World War. Ecclesiastical elements in the village architecture turn up in both likely and unlikely places: the east end of Notre-Dame (below); a chapel-like farmhouse just south of the village (above). Solid villas and wonderfully textured walls grace this crossroads off the Rue Gaston Manneville (opposite).

Preceding pages
The medieval west door of Notre-Dame is surrounded by splendid carving. Another formidable architectural presence is the Halles, facing out across the Place de la République towards the Lieutenancy, former residence of the dukes of Falaise.

Houlgate

There is no shortage of fine houses in the village, from the seaside 'Normanesque' of the Rue des Bains (above) to the half-timbering of the Moulin Landry (opposite) on the Boulevard Jacques Landry, named after a local miller and mayor between 1838 and 1868.

UNLIKE ITS COASTAL NEIGHBOUR, Dives-sur-Mer, just to the west, the village of Houlgate boasts no evidence of fishing fleet or coastal port to suggest that it has ever been anything but what it is now – a holiday resort. But that is not to detract from its charm. Indeed, the very ingenuousness of its bucket-and-spade appeal transports the visitor to a bygone age, when sea-bathing had just come into fashion. The railway was equally brand-new : its ability to whisk a jaded city-dweller from Paris to the coast in two hours must have seemed like science-fiction when the station was built in 1886. Less than thirty years before nothing would have been found there, except wind-swept dunes.

The main street, the Rue des Bains, gives a clue to the first edifice to be erected, a spa establishment whose grand, domed hotel still dominates the eastern end of the village. Shortly afterwards, a smart casino was added to the attractions of the beach, together with a suitably pretentious promenade, named after Roland Garros, a pioneer aviator who took off from the beach here to achieve the world altitude record in September 1912.

Not that the mention of Houlgate's heyday should suggest that today's resort has in any way declined since its boom years. On the contrary, the beach is crowded in the summer season, and for the visitor who has spent enough time admiring the sea, there is the pleasure of a cooling walk along its tree-shaded streets, enjoying glimpses of the richly adorned villas that were built to house the first generation of demurely clad sea-bathers.

*S*easide Normandy : the Rue des Bains runs along the sea front (above)
at Houlgate, viewed here across a sweep of the coastline (opposite)
from the port of Dives-sur-Mer.

Cheese capital of Normandy, Livarot has a fittingly grand setting for its cheese museum in the Manoir de l'Isle (opposite). In the centre of the village the Rue Maréchal Foch climbs to Gothic Saint-Ouen (right)

Livarot

THE NAME OF LIVAROT is a reminder that one is standing at the very centre of the world of cheese. An acquaintance should be respectfully sought with 'Le Colonel', so named for the five straw bands that traditionally bind its ruddy-coloured rind.

In terms of historical maturity, both Livarot (whose *appellation* area actually stretches outside the village as far as Saint-Pierre-sur-Dives) and Pont-l'Évêque, two of the three classic cheeses of Normandy, can look down their noses at the third, produced at Camembert to the south. This is after all an arriviste, invented a mere two centuries ago, its meteoric rise to world fame owing much to new-fangled production methods and bulk shipping to Paris after the arrival of the railway. Pont l'Évêque, however, was praised by connoisseurs of the

thirteenth century, and the pedigree of Livarot can be traced back almost as far. History apart, Livarot, often produced locally on the farm, also smells older, which can put off those unlucky enough not to have got used to its initial 'nose'. An extraordinary quantity of full-cream milk (almost five litres) goes into a 500 gram cheese, so it is understandable that its subsequent creation is not a hasty process. Ageing can take up to a hundred days before the finished article can be wrapped and boxed. Any questions remaining after the educative efforts of the cheese museum, housed in the smart-looking Manoir de l'Isle just outside the village, can be referred to any one of the congenial shopkeepers whose shops line the broad main street which climbs towards the parish church of Saint-Ouen.

*T*he countryside around Livarot is dotted with many delightful
  corners; single houses (opposite) *and whole villages, like Notre-*
Dame-de-Courson (above), *provide a succession of fascinating excursions
from the cheese centre itself.*

Port-en-Bessin

*N*aval actions and then more peaceful fishing have marked the village of Port-en-Bessin, especially around the harbour area, entered through a narrow channel (opposite), *and overlooked by a formidable defensive tower* (below).

ONE EIGHTEENTH-CENTURY VIEW of Port-en-Bessin shows the village squeezed between its two enclosing cliffs, with a tumble of narrow streets trying to accommodate the activities of its population, much as now. The big difference lies in the line of fishing boats on the beach, looking as vulnerable to the weather as the village looks sheltered. It is a tribute to the hardiness and determination of the fishermen of 'Port', as the village is universally known, that theirs was Normandy's most important fishing fleet by the middle years of the eighteenth century.

The constant interruptions of wars against England, however, soon forced those fishermen to look further afield, eventually to deep-sea trawling, at which they excelled. After Napoleon's final defeat, the village became the centre of a busy coastal trade, supplying parts of the coast not yet linked by rail. When the fishing fleet of Trouville, a leading rival, was decimated, not by natural disaster but by the inhabitants' realization that easier money could be made out of tourists than fish, Port grew still further. By this time, a suitably businesslike harbour had been constructed; in keeping with the heavyweight guard-tower placed on the eastern cliff by Vauban two hundred years before, two massive jetties were built to encircle the outer harbour. Today this is full of pleasure craft, while the trawlers bustle through and somehow find space in the new inner harbour, itself crammed into the already restricted village centre. All is activity there, especially on a crowded market-day, but villagers and sailors seem to coexist happily even at close quarters, bound together by the centuries-old traditions of this community of sea-faring folk.

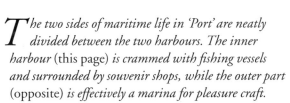

*T*he two sides of maritime life in 'Port' are neatly
divided between the two harbours. The inner
harbour (this page) *is crammed with fishing vessels
and surrounded by souvenir shops, while the outer part*
(opposite) *is effectively a marina for pleasure craft.*

Saint-Pierre-sur-Dives

Village variety: the ornate west end of the abbey church looks on to a tiny square and the local cinema (below); the imposing Mairie, complete with the tricolore, *looks over the Place de l'Hôtel de Ville (opposite).*

SITTING PROUDLY in the huge expanse of Saint-Pierre-sur-Dives' market square, which seethes with activity every Monday morning, the timber-framed Halles is a striking sight. Its huge size is not, in fact, as remarkable as its extreme youth; having faithfully served the community through almost nine hundred years, the original building was destroyed by fire as occupying forces pulled out of the village in August 1944. Extraordinarily, the market hall was rebuilt by the community, keeping strictly to the methods of their eleventh-century predecessors, with not a single nail or staple in the whole building. The wooden pins and pegs that hold the timbers together were all hand-made by one of the local craftsmen. It was re-inaugurated in July 1949, and looks solid enough to stand another nine hundred years, barring accidents.

Such a story of determination overcoming adversity could be said to be part of a tradition in the village. The abbey which once dominated the

*I*t is hard to believe that the imposing 'medieval' Halles (above) *was entirely rebuilt after its destruction in the fighting of 1944. But the traditional methods used have certainly ensured that the final effect is entirely convincing. Equally impressive as village architecture is the tower of the abbey church* (opposite), *rising high above the Hôtel de Ville.*

place, both physically and spiritually, also suffered during its life. Founded in 1012 , first as a convent, it fell victim to the power struggles that followed the death of William the Conqueror. In 1106 it was destroyed by fire. Henry I of England, whose troops were responsible for the arson, paid towards the material costs of repair, but it was the efforts of the local people that ensured its reconstruction. According to accounts of the time, nobles, merchants and peasants alike laboured together, under the leadership of Abbot Haimon, who

sustained their spiritual enthusiasm through what must have been a daunting project (the rebuilding took thirty-nine years) by a series of miracles.

Further misfortune befell the abbey during the Hundred Years War, and again in the Wars of Religion, to say nothing of the final dispersal of the monks by Revolutionary decree in 1790. The main building was preserved as the parish church, however, and plans are afoot to add the charming chapter-house, which also survived, to Saint-Pierre's tally of restored buildings.

Châteaux

*T*he sixteenth-century gatehouse of the Château de Carrouges (Orne) (left) presents a harmonious arrangement of towers and walls, more intimately domestic than defensive. Immediately attractive, too, is the ornately sculpted entrance front of the late-fifteenth-century Château d'O (Orne) (opposite).

FROM MEDIEVAL TIMES, the warlords of Normandy had to seek ducal permission for the construction of a castle – a good way for the dukes to exercise tight control over their nobility and at the same time to develop the defences of the whole region, especially along its southern borders with France. Typically, these early châteaux had only a simple inner keep inside the outer fortifications – suitable habitations only in times of emergency. Later, courtyards surrounded by more spacious residential quarters began to appear.

At Carrouges in Orne, the original rectangular keep, dating from the fourteenth century, was augmented over the centuries to form a sizeable residence. Happily, similar materials, particularly the pink-coloured brick of the locality, were used for each successive remodelling, and the whole now presents a surprisingly coherent, as well as imposing, ensemble.

The Château d'O is bounded by a moat, but presents a gatehouse that is more welcoming than forbidding. The elaborate tracery around the deeply gabled windows strikes a fanciful note echoed throughout this gem of the Renaissance. Its steeply pointed turrets and external walls are patterned with alternating stone and brick.

By the time that Jean-Baptiste-Jacques Élie de Beaumont, successful lawyer and treasurer to the future Charles X, rebuilt his château at Canon, the threat of armed assault must have seemed like a distant nightmare. Beaumont wanted a country retreat in the style of an English gentleman's residence; he was also a friend of Horace Walpole and clearly *au fait* with the latest fashion in garden design, expressed in the elegant wooded park that surrounds his classical château.

The Renaissance walls and towers of the entrance front of the château rise above a moat clearly more of an ornamental feature than an active deterrent to intruders. Later decorative interventions have clearly marked the long gallery (opposite), where the dominant style is distinctly late eighteenth-century.

*M*ore eighteenth-century English than French in style is this tree-planted expanse (above) to the south side of the Château de Canon (Calvados). Its openness is in strict contrast to the same park's series of thirteen enclosed gardens, with connecting arches, known as 'Les Chartreuses' (opposite).

*A*pproached via lanes which meander through the hills of the Suisse
Normande, the Château de Pontécoulant lies in an immaculately cropped
park (opposite). A mixture of sixteenth- and eighteenth-century building, there
is a pleasant eclecticism about the place, typified in the
varied furniture of the main hallway (above).

Orne

Quintessential Normandy, the département of Orne here displays some of its timeless quality: the Tour d'Argentan at Sées (above), last remnant of the town's medieval fortifications; and apples, the raw material of the province's most famous beverages – cider and calvados, at a cider factory near Vimoutiers (opposite).

THE SOUTHERNMOST OF THE FIVE *départements* that make up present-day Normandy, Orne stretches out languorously to the south of its more famous coastal neighbours, Manche and Calvados. A curiosity of the region is that there is no apparent point to it, and certainly no centre. The administrative capital, for example, is the largest town, Alençon. But far from sitting like a fat spider in the midst of things, it dangles absent-mindedly right at the southern fringe, peering over into neighbouring Sarthe. Where the centre should be, close to the source of the river Orne, sits Sées, never besieged, never bombarded, and taking sleepy charm to extremes. A few kilometres away is the region's most famous castle, the Château d'O, not bristling with barbicans and machicolations, but floating serenely on its moat, a vision of Renaissance effortlessness.

Once the visitor has adjusted to the laid-back character of Orne and starts to relish the relaxed atmosphere of the place, its treasures will emerge. Not all are undramatic. Before the river Orne itself, for example, disappears over the border into Calvados, it passes through some of the most extraordinary scenery of its whole length. Such wonders as the Roche d'Oëtre and the Gorges de Saint-Aubert can be enjoyed at leisure by navigating the tiny roads south of Pont-d'Ouilly, where most of the would-be alpinists of the Suisse Normande leave the district on the major road that heads for Falaise.

If the lack of invaders made Orne a peaceful place in past centuries, the absence of huge roads full of thundering lorries is part of its attraction now. The pace of travel is easy, so enough time should be allotted to reach the Perche in the east and explore that dream-like land of forests and rich meadows before returning to sample the most relaxing of Orne's attractions: a curative stay in Bagnoles, with therapeutic woodland walks and health-giving mineral springs.

Bagnoles-de-l'Orne

LIKE ANY self-respecting spa resort, Bagnoles-de-l'Orne has a long tradition of trumpeting the claims of its curative regimes. The arrival of the railway in 1869 first started to multiply the number of visitors; enticing posters showed off its wooded valley and the smart new Établissement Thermal in the Paris termini, luring the weary commuter away from the stresses of a city existence.

The history of Bagnoles as a resort did not start with the brain-wave of a nineteenth- century entrepreneur, however. Many centuries before, the particular qualities of the water attracted seasonal *curistes* who 'took the waters' and recuperated in the good air and peaceful ambience of the valley. There was even an entirely appropriate legend attached to the place, which told of a knight returning from a faraway campaign with his worn-out war-horse which, on account of its loyalty, he could not bring himself to put to death and so let wander into the forest. It was found later miraculously restored, having bathed in a spring in the woods, and its joyous owner, having followed its example, began a merry retirement with a new young wife, who bore him copious offspring.

A sceptic might detect a certain made-to-measure feel about the story, and date it to the time of the railway posters, but what is a legend if not a primitive variety of advertising? At least its claims seem to have been true: the water itself, bubbling up at 30 degrees centigrade underneath the huge Établissement, can boast an analysis of its mineral content running to several 'scientific' pages, while the therapeutic benefits of its setting can be tested in a single morning by any visitor who takes a stroll in the steps of the legendary war-horse through the charming woodland which has been preserved close to the main spa centre.

The shady avenues, lined with 'Normanesque' hotels and villas from the boom years of the railway age, are equally enticing. In the evening, after a hearty meal, more diversions can be enjoyed among the throngs who visit the Casino, sited beside the toy-like lake to dance and play the slot-machines with all the gusto of the truly rejuvenated.

The splendidly adorned and decorated Place de la République (above) lies near the lake of Bagnoles. At its head is the Pavillon du Moulin (opposite), one of the many establishments catering for the needs of the many visitors who take the waters in this charming spa.

*V*illas and hotels are the necessary architectural accompaniment
to the life of a spa, from the splendid Résidence du Lac (right)
to the Chalet Suedois (above) *on the Boulevard Albert-Christophe.
The latter was in fact originally built for the 1889 Paris Exhibition,
then moved in its entirety to its present location.*

Bellême

ON THE EASTERN EXTREMITIES of the Orne *département*, the thickly forested hills of the Perche divide the varied countryside of the Orne and the flat, wheat-growing plains of the Beauce beyond. Undulating in terrain and idiosyncratic in character, the Perche has become famous for two widely differing reasons: Percheron horses and Trappist monks. The area immediately around Bellême provides a third speciality, perhaps more attractive to the casual visitor: a profusion of rare and delicious mushrooms. Above the woods through which visiting mycologists snuffle during each September's international Mycologiade, Bellême rises to its proud height of 225 metres, enough to dominate the neighbouring landscape even without the addition, in the Middle Ages, of a fortress-citadel.

This was besieged, in 1229, by the Regent, Blanche of Castile (the royal camp-site is still marked two kilometres from the village by the Carrefour de la Croix-Feue-Reine) and the official commander-in-chief, her eleven-year-old son Louis, who later became the crusading Louis IX. The assault was successful and the pro-English Pierre de Mauclerc dislodged.

His castle has disappeared, except for a hefty fortified gatehouse, complete with portcullis mountings, on the way from the very peaceable main square into the Rue Ville Close, where seventeenth- and eighteenth-century houses were built inside the ramparts of the old castle. Many of them survive in fine condition, the most magnificent, the Hôtel de Bansard des Bois, which shows off its stylish rear elevation to the outside world through a reflection in the remains of the castle moat. Such seigneurial airs have perhaps lent weight to Bellême's claim to be called the capital of the Perche, despite centuries of disagreement with its larger neighbour, the market-town of Mortagne-au-Perche, ten kilometres to the north.

*T*he eighteenth-century Hôtel de Bansard des Bois, in the Rue Ville Close, is by far the most stylish house in Bellême, viewed here from the boulevard of the same name.

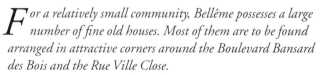

For a relatively small community, Bellême possesses a large number of fine old houses. Most of them are to be found arranged in attractive corners around the Boulevard Bansard des Bois and the Rue Ville Close.

This community is dominated by its château, although it is the village itself which occupies the higher ground (opposite). *Below it, the buildings of the great house are truly magnificent: the great staircase has fine brick vaulting* (above), *and the gatehouse* (right) *is a substantial edifice in its own right.*

Carrouges

FEW OF THE BUILDINGS in the hilltop village of Carrouges can boast any great antiquity, and certainly none are as old as the great château which bears the name of the village. Such a famous and imposing edifice, dating from the fourteenth century, would normally dominate the village in which it stands. Carrouges is an exception: the village on the hilltop looks down on the château, which sits in a moat at the foot of the Udon valley. The château is not the only attraction in Carrouges – a former chapter-house is now the visitor centre for the Parc Naturel Régional Normandie-Maine, which includes the Forêt d'Écouves, of which Carrouges is the capital.

Down the hill from the village centre, the approach to the château leads past orchards towards the four pointed turrets and lively decorative brickwork of a sixteenth-century gatehouse. Its playful appearance in no way detracts from the powerful impact of the château itself, rising gracefully from its not-quite-square island in the middle of a balustraded moat. The outside walls, built mainly of a mixture of brick and granite, are remarkably of a piece, considering that the entrance front facing west is part of a fourteenth-century keep and that the remaining additions enclosing the central courtyard were built in the reign of Henri IV, by which time château styles had evolved from fortress to *demeure de plaisance*.

Inside, the layout is as if rearranged for the life of a noble family of the seventeenth century: its members lived on the first floor, while the kitchens

The houses of the village centre (above) *occupy the crest of the hill which overlooks the château. Below, the latter's charming park stretches out along the valley floor of the Udon* (opposite).

and domestic offices conducted their business below. Between the floors, the main staircase is presented in its bare brickwork, its covering of plaster quite stripped away, a surprise at first, but a good chance to appreciate the intricacy of its structure. The Le Veneur family lived there for more than four hundred years before finally bequeathing the property to the State in 1936.

Domfront

COMMANDINGLY SITED on a lofty ridge of limestone, Domfront has the same air of impregnability as the *bastide* towns of the Périgord – indeed it was the renowned hermit from that region, St. Front, who founded a religious settlement in the Passais countryside nearby and left it his name. The village's rocky perch is in fact part of a ridge that runs from Mortain east to Carrouges. At Domfront, the south-running river Varenne has cut a gorge through the ridge, leaving a third side of the village protected by a sheer slope. Successive Norman noblemen added to the first *donjon* at this end of the village, and houses were grouped along the ridge. Henry Beauclerck, later King Henry I of England, took the place over and used it as his base to overcome the efforts of his brother Robert to hold on to the Norman lands he had purloined from their father. Once Robert had been defeated and captured at Tinchebray in 1106, Henry became king of both England and Normandy. He set up his court at Domfront, as did his successors. His son, Henry II, particularly liked the place, bringing his queen, Eleanor of Aquitaine, and their court of troubadours and poets there. In the calmer days of his relationship with Thomas à Becket, the archbishop joined his king here and celebrated mass in the church of Notre-Dame-de-l'Eau on Christmas Day, 1166. It was also there, four years later, that a papal legation attempted to negotiate a settlement between the two men, in vain.

Nothing of the castle of the Henrys survives now, except two portions of the main *donjon*, which give an idea of its massive scale, and the stumps of two towers that protected the curtain walls on the village side. The whole castle, including later fortifications and a chapel, was fated to meet a sudden end: it was blown up in 1608, by order of Henry IV's minister Sully.

The defences around the older part of the village were left alone, however – especially fortunate for those houses which were actually built into the walls during the 15th century. Much of the old perimeter wall is still intact, and a stroll along the Rue des Fossés-Plisson, which runs along its south flank, gives an excellent view of it, including seven of its eleven remaining towers. Most strolls end up in the park that now encloses the castle remains. From here the wonderful views, as well as the size of the castle ruins, give us some idea of the grand scale of the place in its heyday.

A surprising view in a village of Domfront's antiquity is that of the 1924 neo-Byzantine façade of the church of Saint-Julien (above). More typical of the place are the venerable houses built into the old defensive walls (opposite).

Saint-Céneri-le-Gérei

DRAMATIC despite its tiny scale, Saint-Céneri hangs above the river Sarthe, which meanders between steep, wooded banks as it makes its way south from Alençon. The village, as well as the river, almost flows into the neighbouring *départements*, finding itself just in Orne, but within a few hundred metres both of Sarthe and Mayenne.

From the 11th century a château dominated this border position from a plug of hard rock, around which the river Sarthe twists, giving defenders complete command of the crossing below. This stronghold was built by the local family of the Giroie (or Gérei) to resist the constant pillaging of the Normans. It was besieged both by William the Conqueror, and by his son Henry. The Giroie clan also built the small, plain Romanesque church that occupies the same high bluff, overlooking the river. A little path round the back of its semi-circular apse gives an excellent view down to the eleventh-century stone bridge and the old stone houses clustered around it. Also in the churchyard stand two chimney-pieces – the only remnants of the château.

It was the English who finally managed a successful siege, during the Hundred Years War, with the aid of cannon mounted on a crag opposite. Thereafter, the fortunes of the village relied on the availability of iron ore and plentiful supplies of wood, which kept artisanship alive in its forges until the end of the nineteenth century. By then, the lure of its picturesque situation had brought a regular colony of artists, following in the footsteps of Jean-Baptiste Corot, who fell in love with the village on his first visit here in 1855.

*M*uch loved by painters, this picturesque village is bisected by the river Sarthe.

The attraction of Saint-Céneri for artists becomes easily explicable when its many charming details start to reveal themselves (this page). An added advantage is its location on the banks of the Sarthe, here glimpsed from the old village bridge as it flows past a former mill (opposite).

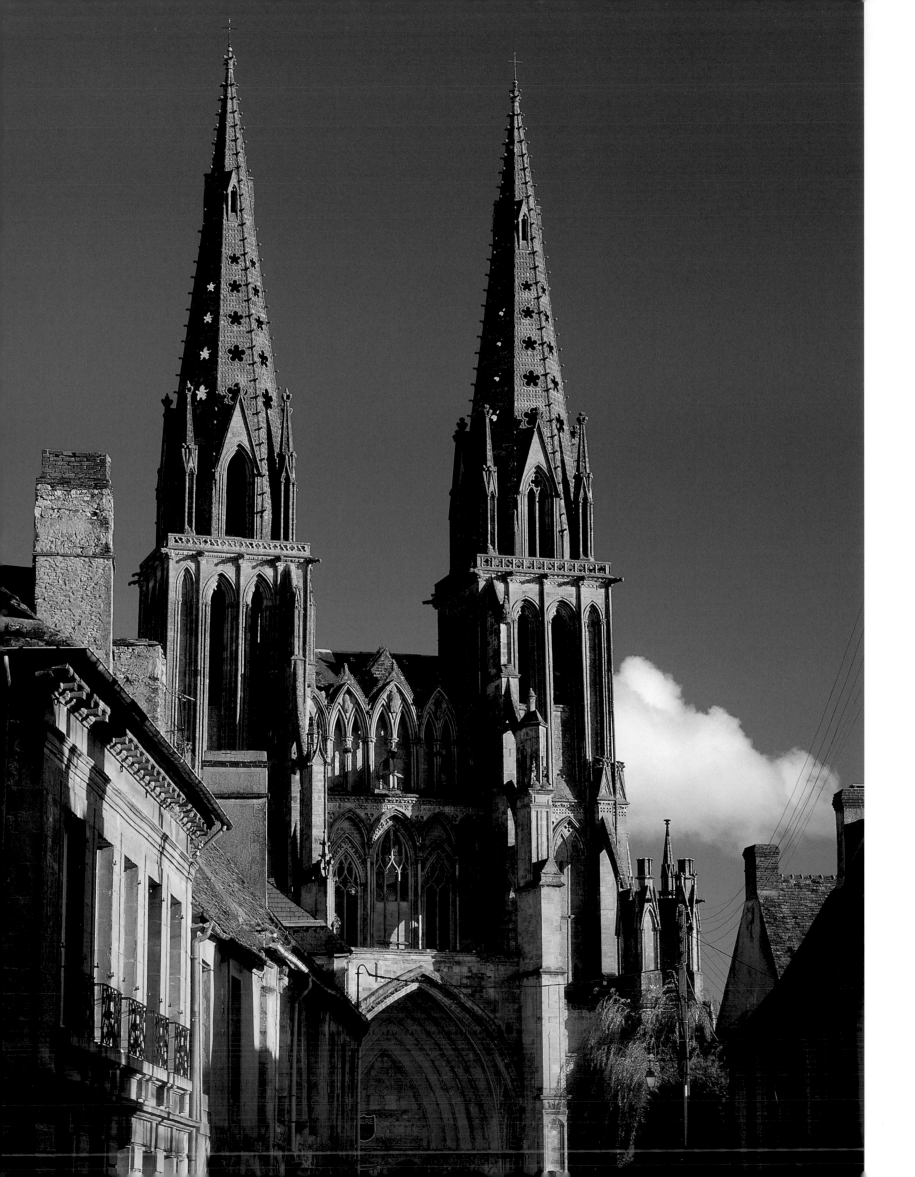

Sées

The nineteenth-century Gothic Revival spires of the cathedral, rising above the thirteenth-century west front (opposite), *strike a grand note in contrast to the more modest, though engagingly attractive dwellings of the village* (below).

THE SOUTHERN REACHES of Normandy, near its historical border with France, are the kind of place where you might expect to find a bristling, defensive citadel. Instead, tucked away on the edge of the Forêt d'Écouves and bordering fields of wheat to the north, sits tranquil Sées. A certain wistful air about it may be explained by a falling-off in the demand for its staple product – religion. On approaching the marvellous collection of ecclesiastical buildings at its centre, however, it is difficult not to feel a sense of spirituality in the place. But despite its appearance, the history of Sées has not been entirely uneventful

– the present cathedral is not the first church to stand in its place. In fact, it is the fifth.

The first of the cathedrals fell victim to a Saxon raid in 878; the second lasted barely one hundred years before it suffered a similar fate. After twenty years of rebuilding, the cathedral of Azon the Venerable was consecrated, but lasted only forty years. Azon's successor, Yves de Bellême, decided to flush out a band of brigands from the cathedral precincts by setting fire to neighbouring houses. He lived to regret this stratagem: the cathedral was also burnt to the ground and, at the Council of Reims

*F*rom the Rue d'Argentan another neo-Gothic monument is visible: the church of the Immaculate Conception (above *and* opposite). *Built in 1854, it was finally consecrated in 1879. Just in front of its west front stands a remaining vestige of Sées' fortifications – the round Tour d'Argentan.*

the following year, the Bishop had to account for himself to the Pope. Charged with rebuilding, Yves set off on a fund-raising expedition that took him all the way through Italy, and as far as Constantinople. He returned to Sées and commenced work in 1060. It would be satisfying to report that after his long period of prayer and mortification, he was divinely inspired to be the first rebuilder to choose a less flammable medium than wood. Alas, such was not the case, and after over sixty years of building, the fourth cathedral lasted less than fifty years before it

met the same fate (mercifully not in the lifetime of the miserable Yves).

The later medium of choice was stone, and it is the thirteenth-century masterpiece of Norman Gothic that has survived to this day. The light-coloured Chailloué limestone, soft to work but hardening as it ages, was used for the whole building. The interior is possessed of a wonderful luminosity, not least because of the scale and scope of its original stained-glass.

*H*alf-timbering in the Normandy *départements was the traditional method of construction for the more unpretentious rural buildings* (left), *here at Domfront (Orne). Later, it was used for more elaborate houses as a revivalist style, as in this example at Bagnoles-de-l'Orne* (opposite).

NORMANDY'S FONDNESS for half-timbered construction is evident not only in the large number of traditional buildings lovingly preserved until the present day, but also in the way that more recent architects and builders have continued to use the same technique purely for decorative effect. Naturally, this way of building first evolved according to the availability of materials and to known building technology.

Stone was often too costly and too difficult to obtain to be used for the average domestic or agricultural building. Walls were typically built either from cob, made from a mixture of clay and gravel, bound together with straw or horse-hair, or from clay puddled with water and bound with chopped straw. The wooden framework of uprights and horizontal beams was usually laid out on the ground, pegged together and raised to sit on top of the stone or brick footings that prevented the walls from rotting from the dampness of the ground. The cob mixture would then be packed between the beams. Later variations saw the use of tiles or bricks stacked between the beams, often in decorative herringbone patterns.

The roofs of such houses or barns would be made of tiles, slates or thatch, depending on the materials of the neighbourhood. In the areas where thatch was used, it is not uncommon to see a neat row of irises growing along the roof ridge. These were traditionally planted in the clay along the ridge apex, so that their roots could bind the clay together and prevent it from drying out.

Half-timbered Buildings

*G*ustave Flaubert chose a village of traditional brick and half-
timbered buildings (Ry, in Seine-Maritime) as the original for the
setting of Madame Bovary (opposite). *In Dives-sur-Mer (Calvados)*
(above) *the half-timbered building has a distinctly late-medieval air.*

These pages
*P*articularly fine examples of
half-timbering grace the main
street of Ry (Seine-Maritime),
evoking in a very real way the
village setting of Madame Bovary.

Overleaf
*T*he area around the village of
Le Bec-Hellouin (Eure)
and along the valley of the Risle
will reward the visitor with many
fine examples of half-timbering:
here, in Le Bec-Hellouin itself,
and at Brionne-Saint-Denis.

Eure

The département of Eure, lying across one of the main pilgrimage routes of Europe, has a long tradition of religious activity. This carving (above), in a fifteenth-century rest-house in Conches-en-Ouche, would have greeted pilgrims on their way to Compostela in northern Spain. In Le Bec-Hellouin, the abbey grounds look towards an impressive and well-endowed parish church (opposite).

PARISIANS have always nurtured a special, sentimental affection for Normandy – a land of riches, whose produce they have enjoyed at their tables, and a countryside of beauty, which they have loved to visit. Of Normandy's five *départements*, Eure lies closest to the capital. It was just inside its borders, a mere fifty-five kilometres from Paris, that Claude Monet discovered his beloved, peaceful Giverny. The rest of this part of the region, lying to the north of the Seine, is no less rustic; Lyons-la-Forêt, for instance, sits in the middle of Normandy's largest expanse of forest. South of the Seine, almost all of the lower half of the Eure was once forest; it was only in the late Middle Ages that its clearance started to intensify, releasing the great expanses of fertile farmland around Saint-André and Le Neubourg.

Even without the trees, there is nothing bare about these plains. A network of streams criss-crosses the country between the larger rivers of the Eure, the Iton and the Risle. Substantial remnants of forest also lie to the west, beside Conches and Beaumont-le-Roger. An indication of the slow pace of change in this part of Normandy is the retention in private hands of the forest of Beaumont, which covers no less than 4000 hectares. A sublime example of Baroque architecture, a rarity in Normandy, stands nearby – the great château of Beaumesnil. The Risle itself runs more or less due north to meet the Seine almost at the end of its course at Le Havre.

The rich pasturage of this valley brought considerable wealth to many of the communities dotted along its course. Brionne, which actually straddles the river, was considered a rich enough prize for William the Conqueror to spend almost two years besieging it. Much of the northern Eure has come under the protection of the Parc Naturel Régional de Brotonne, which has helped this largely agricultural area retain its charm. Many of the buildings are thatched, and the apple orchards contain ancient fruit varieties saved from extinction.

Conches-en-Ouche

The unassuming edifices devoted to ecclesiastical matters in Conches seem to have survived in rather better shape than their more immediately grand secular counterparts. The ruins of the twelfth-century castle loom over the valley of the Rouloir (opposite); suitably retiring, in contrast, is the pilgrim's rest-house in the Rue Sainte-Foy (below).

DOMINATING the southern plain of the Pays d'Ouche from its commanding limestone spur, Conches has an air of being of some consequence. It was first significant as the southern outpost of a family fiefdom, that of the powerful Tosny clan. The first *seigneur* of this family to settle here was Roger de Tosny, whose son fought alongside Duke William as his standard-bearer at the Battle of Hastings. Roger reputedly gave Conches its name on his return from a campaign against the Moors in Spain in 1034. During his journey home, he stopped at Conques in the far south, to which pilgrims had been flocking since the cult of the child-saint St. Foy had established itself there. Moved by piety or entrepreneurship, or some mixture of the two, Roger 'acquired' (in the demure words of the history books) some of the saintly relics of Conques, and

returned home to found a northern outpost of the cult – at Conques-en-Ouche, which later became known as Conches.

The church of Sainte-Foy, thus renamed by Roger, was largely rebuilt at the end of the fifteenth century. The west front of this huge church, which contains some of northern France's most celebrated stained-glass, gives straight on to the main street, opposite a lovely group of medieval houses, some with vaulted and labyrinthine chambers to be explored below ground. Emerging from the spine-challenging dungeon-like lower levels of the Maison Saint-Jacques, the visitor has a pleasant choice: a stroll between the seven *allées* of trees that form the stately park nearby, or a seat on the terrace beside the church of Sainte-Foy, to enjoy the view over the Pays d'Ouche.

*T*he highly decorated spire of the church of Sainte-Foy (above left) *soars above the more modest dwellings of the village* (left). *In the main street the west front of the church* (above) *is a powerful presence. Pleasantly wooded grounds surround the stretch of water known as the Grand' Mare* (opposite), *seen here from the Place Général de Gaulle.*

Fontaine-l'Abbé

THE QUIET D133, heading east from Bernay, follows the picturesque course of the Charentonne, as it makes its way along a verdant, flat-bottomed valley to join the Risle at Serquigny. Several rather stylish water-mills come into view along the river's course - they date from the nineteenth century, but long before they were built, its now peaceful banks would have resounded to the roaring of furnaces and the clang of hammer on anvil. Iron ore was found all over the Pays d'Ouche, and from medieval times many settlements along this part of the Charentonne supported workshops and forges, making use of the plentiful supply of timber, and of course the harnessed power of the stream itself.

Fontaine-l'Abbé itself is tucked away on the other side of the river, slightly aloof from the more workmanlike roadside hamlets of Camfleur and Courcelles, which make up the rest of its commune. The 'Abbé' in the name derives from the former ownership of the village by the Benedictine abbey at Bernay; the first lay *seigneurs* of the village were members of the Fontaine family, and it was their descendants who in the early seventeenth century built the château behind the church, resplendent in alternating stripes of brick and flintwork.

Behind it rise wooded hills, which mark the northern edge of the huge forest of Beaumont, a 4000-hectare expanse, still full of game, and still in private ownership. The church, dedicated to St. John the Baptist, and topped with an imposing nineteenth-century brick tower, adjoins the park of the château, whose huge circular *pigeonnier* looms above the graveyard.

Viewed from the west, the village church, dedicated to Saint John the Baptist, and the seventeenth-century château make an interesting pairing of the ecclesiastical and the secular.

Giverny

EXPLORING the peaceful riverside hamlet of Giverny, it comes as something of a surprise to realize that Paris is a mere 55 kilometres away. It is not hard, however, to imagine this tranquil place catching the sharp eye of the painter Claude Monet as his train rattled by, taking him on one of his many painting expeditions to the Normandy coast. He rented a house and started to put down his roots there, surrounded by his large family, discovering in the locality a rich inspiration for his work. The haystacks immortalized in his 1890 series of paintings were found in the fields around the village, and at the foot of his garden was the river Epte, on which he regularly set out at dawn in a canoe, fascinated by the evanescent effects of light and water.

By 1892 the efforts of his dealers in Paris began to match his prodigious output, and he became wealthy enough to buy the property. From this time until the end of his life, Monet refined his vision and delved ever deeper into the subject-matter that he found around him. The obsessive pursuit of his painting (details of his daily creative regimen are fascinating, if exhausting, to read) was, especially towards the end of his long life, counter-balanced by the comparatively slower business of creating a

The Hôtel Baudy, once frequented by Monet and his friends, stands in the Rue Claude Monet. Behind it, in the garden, is an atelier for the use of passing painters.

*F*ollowing Monet's inspiration, the householders of Giverny seem determined to fill every available space with flowers (above *and* opposite).

garden. He bought enough land to create his famous water garden, whose lilies alone inspired no less than 250 paintings and which, complete with moon bridge, wisterias and weeping willows, became an incarnation of the Japanese prints he so admired. Monet lived on, battling with failing eyesight but productive to the last, to the grand old age of 86. He was buried in the churchyard of Sainte-Radégonde, which lies alongside the main street which now bears his name.

Gardens, long in the making, unfortunately deteriorate faster than paintings and, by the time the property passed to the State in 1966, it was a picture of sad decline. The determination of the first curator, Gérald van der Kemp, that the gardens should be restored to the famously exacting standards of their creator, has given the visitor today a wonderful treat – and many thousands do make the pilgrimage here each year to admire the characterful legacy that Monet created.

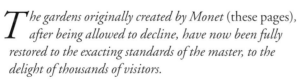

*T*he gardens originally created by Monet (these pages), after being allowed to decline, have now been fully restored to the exacting standards of the master, to the delight of thousands of visitors.

*H*ardly needing the aid of a verbal description, the walled garden is one of the chief glories of the Jardins Claude Monet.

Le Bec-Hellouin

DRIVING NORTHWARDS from the quiet town of Brionne, along the Risle valley, it is easy to miss a small lane to the right, which meanders alongside one of the Risle's smaller tributaries, the Bec. A peaceful place even now, a thousand years ago it must have been the perfect retreat for Herluin, a Brionne knight who was seeking somewhere to lead a life of religious contemplation. By 1042, there were thirty-two monks in his community, and they were shortly joined by one of the most remarkable men of his generation, the Italian-born scholar Lanfranc.

Brionne in those days was important enough to warrant a two-year siege, conducted by the rising force in politics and military might in Normandy, Duke William. During this period William and Lanfranc met and a friendship developed between them. Recognizing that the monk's talents and connections could smooth his uneasy relations with the church, William persuaded him to leave the abbey and join his court. It was Lanfranc who travelled to Rome to secure the annulment of the papal interdict dating from William's marriage to Matilda. In 1070, he became Archbishop of Canterbury, with papal approval. Before he left his beloved abbey, he appointed a fellow Italian, his pupil Anselm, to be its prior. Later, Anselm also became Archbishop of Canterbury – though unwillingly.

Following these two great scholars, the monks and their pupils (one of whom became Pope Alexander II), guided the abbey into a central role in the intellectual life of northern Europe. Physically, too, it grew to fill its present large walled domain. Most of the monastic buildings date from the seventeenth century. Of the original church, only the detached bell-tower still stands – the Tour Saint-Nicolas, whose 201 steps can be climbed to give a commanding view of the pretty adjoining village, the small stream of the Bec, and its wide and verdant valley.

A place of charm, with traditional architecture in abundance (opposite), this village is also heir to an important European ecclesiastical heritage, continued most immediately by its parish church (above).

*T*he Tour Saint-Nicolas (opposite *and* overleaf) *literally towers above the attractive streets and dwellings of the village; the last important remnant of the old abbey, it yields splendid views over the Bec valley. Beneath it lie the details of the village and the land adjoining the river* (this page).

Lyons-la-Forêt

*T*he timbered Halles on Place *Isaac de Bensérade (opposite) is the scene of a lively market in this village of literary, cinematic and musical associations. Maurice Ravel is said to have composed* Le Tombeau de Couperin *in the Maison 'Le Fresne' on the Rue d'Enfer (below).*

THE FOREST OF LYONS, which spreads massively over the undulating plain to the east of Rouen, is Normandy's largest; it can also rightly claim to be its most prestigious, for the excellence of the hunting here exerted a powerful draw for generations of royalty. Sited in a clearing at its centre, Lyons-la-Forêt can regard itself (something it likes to do) as the capital of the forest. Despite its tiny size, the preponderance of traditional timbered houses, mostly from the seventeenth century, and their excellent condition, give it an air of importance, with all the grace of a regional centre but with none of the bustle. Visitors are present in great numbers, inevitably, and two masters of the French cinema, Jean Renoir and Claude Chabrol, have used the pretty timbered Halles and the fine collection of houses around the main square as the backdrop for their versions of Flaubert's *Madame Bovary*, whose real-life heroine lived her tempestuous life nearby.

On the knoll that distinguishes Lyons' location from other clearings in the forest, a grand stone keep was built by the dukes of Normandy in the twelfth century, and the village grew up around it. The castle has entirely disappeared, but its position is clear on a map: right in the middle of the village a circle of green is enclosed by an almost perfect ring of stone houses. These earliest houses, which at first enjoyed the shelter of the castle walls, present an understandably smug face to the passing world: after the castle was pulled down, their stylish façades, many rebuilt with stone from the castle ruins, have kept their inordinately large gardens secret from the envious gaze of all but the birds. On the way down to the church of Saint-Denis, which stands a little way from the village, is an inscribed stele, commemorating a royal death. For it was here in Lyons, after a day's hunting in November 1135, that Henry I expired.

*I*t is small wonder that Lyons-
la-Forêt is a favourite setting
for film-makers, for the number
of attractive houses is astonishing
for such a small place: *from the
Rue Derrière-les-Jardins* (above
left); *the Rue du Trou Grenu*
(above right); *behind the main
square* (opposite); *and in the
Sentiers des Trois Moulins* (left).
The three mills referred to in the
street name, seen here, were in the
direct ownership of the French
royal family until the Revolution;
they continued to provide the
village with electricity until the
Second World War.

Nonancourt

AFTER HENRY BEAUCLERCK, Duke William's third son and later King Henry I of England, had defeated his brother Robert and regained his father's Norman territories, he set about securing his new possessions. As well as the unbrotherly but necessary tactic of keeping Robert gaoled for the remaining twenty-eight years of his life, he took care to fortify the dukedom's borders with France. One of the settlements he strengthened in 1112 along the natural southern frontier of the river Avre was Nonancourt, along with its western neighbours, Tillières and Verneuil. Philippe of France had allied himself with Robert, and Henry correctly judged that his Capetian heirs would be no more trustworthy. They in turn fortified Saint-Rémy on their side of the river, and Nonancourt was witness to displays of military force and the occasional short-lived truce.

Sufficient lengths of the defensive walls, with their stout round towers, survive to provide an interesting backdrop to a stroll above the village, which slopes down towards the Avre. The river divides here to flow past the old mills and warehouses along the Quai Henri IV. In the central Place Aristide Briand, a good number of old half-timbered houses are congregated by the west front of the church of Saint-Martin, whose lofty octagonal clock-tower sports an unusual *galerie* of wood, decorated with curious carvings, one portraying a bearded man, with a basket of fruit on his head. Beyond the river lies the village of Saint-Lubin, with its own smaller church. The two villages now form a single commune, and the little bridges that link them are scarcely noticeable. It is somehow satisfying to learn, however, that less than a hundred years ago an inhabitant of Nonancourt, heading over the river to Saint-Lubin, would have echoed the sentiments of his king of a thousand years before, with the utterance: 'I am going to France'.

*T*he streets around the church of Saint-Martin in
this former fortress (opposite) are full of
atmosphere strangely not of the present. The church
itself is notable for its octagonal belfry (right),
peering above the pleasant little details of domestic
architecture in neighbouring streets and alleys
(below *and* foot of page).

Churches and Abbeys

A beacon of militant Christianity, a flood-lit Mont-Saint-Michel (Manche) (left) rises up from the polders at dusk. Inside, the Knights' Hall (opposite), home of the Order of the Knights of St. Michael, was also used as the monks' scriptorium, thus neatly symbolizing the dual importance of the mount.

MANY DIFFERENT ARCHITECTURAL STYLES are to be found in the great churches and abbeys of Normandy. In those of great antiquity a combination of styles from successive periods will almost certainly be revealed. Such is the case with Normandy's famous island landmark, Mont-Saint-Michel. The original eleventh-century church was incorporated as a crypt (Notre-Dame-sous-Terre) beneath the nave of the present church. Here, the fascinating vertical progression through the centuries turns to the horizontal, as the solidly sombre Romanesque nave leads into the airy elegance of the Gothic chancel. The most striking additions made in the Gothic style are the collection of buildings to the north side, collectively known as 'La Merveille'. It is these that give the mount its extraordinary, almost otherworldly, outline.

Of equal antiquity, but sadly in ruins, is the great abbey at Jumièges, tucked into a loop of the Seine not far from Rouen. This was built by William Longsword, son of Rollo, the first Duke of Normandy, on the site of a seventh-century abbey destroyed by his Viking forebears. Enough remains of the vast abbey church, first consecrated by William the Conqueror in 1067, to give an idea of the scale and importance of the abbey in its heyday.

A superb example of the Flamboyant Gothic style can be seen at Caudebec-en-Caux, formerly the capital of the Pays de Caux, where the church of Notre-Dame adjoins the venerable market-place. The extraordinary west end dates from the end of the fifteenth century; it has three highly decorated doorways.

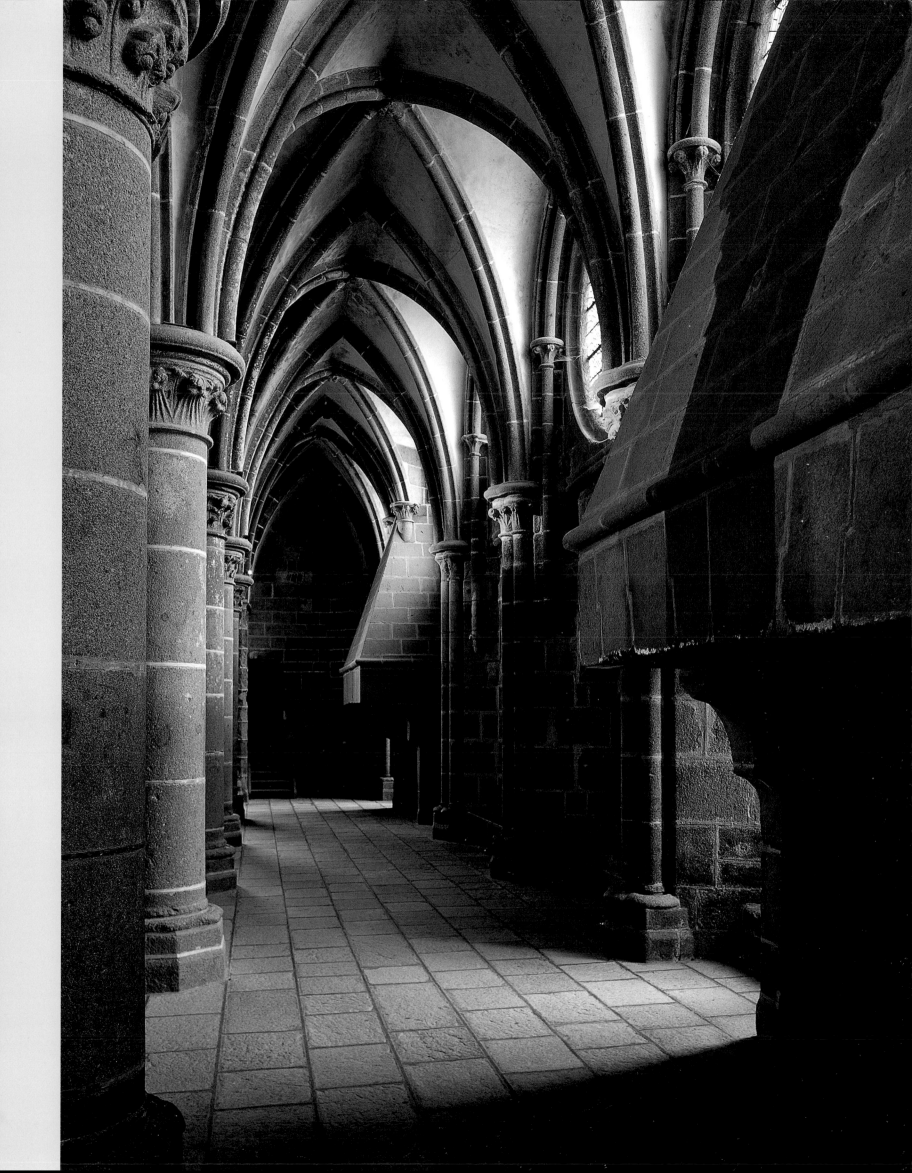

*O*ne *of the most impressive monuments of the whole of Normandy, the ruined abbey of Jumièges (Seine-Maritime) (left) still impresses by its sheer scale and the grandeur of its imperfection. Dynamited after the Revolution to facilitate the dispersal of its stone, the remains of the abbey, including the two huge towers, were eventually saved from final destruction in the mid nineteenth century. More modest in scale is the Romanesque gem of Notre-Dame at Étretat (Seine-Maritime) (above), once a dependency of the abbey of Fécamp.*

Now a house of retreat, the Abbaye Blanche at Mortain (Manche) is another medieval survivor, although only the southern part of the cloister remains (overleaf). The Romanesque part, the transept crossing, of Notre-Dame at Dives-sur-Mer (Calvados), part of the church originally founded by William the Conqueror as thanksgiving for his victory in England, was engulfed by the more elaborate Gothic of the centuries which followed (p.163).

*T*he exquisite Flamboyant Gothic tracery of Notre-Dame (opposite)
at Caudebec-en-Caux, near Villequier (Seine-Maritime), caused
Henri IV to describe it as 'the most beautiful chapel in the kingdom'. In
the same chapel, a magnificent sixteenth-century stained-glass window
shows well-known Biblical scenes (above).

Seine-Maritime

Two facets of a département: *carved detail from the church of Saint-Martin, Harfleur* (above); *inland, the château of Bailleul languishes peacefully in its mature park* (opposite).

ONE-HUNDRED-AND-TWENTY kilometres of coastline, celebrated for its outstanding beauty, runs between Seine-Maritime's two famous ports, Le Havre and Dieppe. This was the first coast to be colonized by Parisian holidaymakers after the railway linked the capital to its nearest beaches. It also saw the birth of an artistic movement: Monet's canvas, *Impression, soleil levant,* painted near Le Havre and exhibited in 1872, gave rise to the term 'Impressionist', first coined by a Parisian critic as one of disparagement. Inland from the Côte d'Albâtre, as this famous stretch of chalk cliffs is called, meandering valleys weave their way inland, uncovering ancient châteaux beside quiet villages.

These valleys, of the Durdent and the Saâne, the Varenne and the Scie, trace ribbons of green through the Pays de Caux, the vast level prairie of arable land that lies in a triangle between the coast and the forested valley of the Seine. Exposed to the constant ravages of the westerly wind, the fields of the Pays de Caux are protected by huge earth embankments, planted with thick hedges of beech, oak and ash. The farmsteads and their hamlets of outbuildings, dotted over the prairie-like expanses like oases, are often surrounded by complete four-square screens of trees.

Between Dieppe and Paris, the flat and treeless plain merges with the rich pastureland of the Pays de Bray, home of the famous heart-shaped Neufchâtel cheese. This land is wooded, but not on the same scale as the Seine valley itself, where the huge river loops its way round the massive and ancient forests of Roumare and the Trait Maulévrier. On the fringes of these rich woodlands, and benefiting from the Seine's course between the capital and the sea, river ports were established, and two outstanding abbeys whose foundation can be traced back to the 7th century: Jumièges and Saint-Wandrille.

Beauvoir-en-Lyons

Now usually converted to dwellings, several of the large half-timbered buildings of the village (above and opposite) were originally glass-making ateliers.

AFTER A DRIVE from the coast through the bare expanses of the Caux plateau, the hills and dales of the Pays de Bray offer a relief to the senses. Not that the verdancy of the countryside has made it more prosperous in farming terms – the windswept plains of the Caux have always been productive in cereals, thanks to the layer of rich silt that lies on top of the limestone. The Bray countryside is wooded and green, lying mainly in a vast clay-bottomed depression, the famous 'Bray buttonhole', which runs from northwest to southeast, from Neufchâtel down towards Beauvais. This was the result of a gigantic geological accident, which left the clay-filled hollow bounded by irregular chalk cliffs and outcrops.

On one of these heights sits Beauvoir-en-Lyons, its favoured position ample justification for its ancient name. In the times of the Norman dukes there was a castle here, positioned close to the present church of Saint-Nicolas, which took full advantage of the 'fine view' indicated in the village name. The French king Philippe-Auguste destroyed the castle after gaining control of Normandy, together with many others which had offered defiance.

Beauvoir itself benefited later from the glass-making industry that grew up in the nearby forest of Lyons from the 13th century onwards. Traces of ancient glassworks can still be found in some of the huge timbered buildings dotted about the village, which once housed workshops and furnaces, subsequently converted into barns. The centre of Beauvoir has an amply proportioned main street, reflecting its past importance, though the village's present-day charm depends very much on the peace and quiet of the place. The fine view remains, however, and it is worth strolling down beside the ancient church to admire the wide green Bray valley stretching away towards Beauvais. On a clear day its cathedral can be seen, fifty kilometres away.

CLÈRES sits in the narrow valley of the little Clérette, its main street following the course of the tiny brook so closely that its ancient Halles almost dips its feet in the water. A series of dainty footbridges links the two rows of shops that face each other over the main square, where brick, flint and wood form an attractive combination in the façades of many of the older houses. At either end of the village, the winding valley's steep sides are thickly wooded, the haven until the mid 19th

century for packs of wolves. Nowadays, animal encounters in Clères are a tamer but still interesting affair, with the exotic beasts that roam the Jean Delacour zoological garden in the park of the village château.

A scientist of world renown in the field of botany as well as ornithology, Jean Delacour started his first zoo at his parents' house in Picardy before the First World War. War damage rendered that property more or less uninhabitable both for the

Clères

The château and its park (opposite) *by the river Clérette are home to the famous Jean Delacour zoological garden. The tiny river flows beneath dainty little bridges through the village itself* (right), *home of some remarkable examples of traditional Norman half-timbering* (above).

Clères is a compilation of varied building materials and styles: nineteenth-century decorative brickwork (above), eighteenth-century timbering in the market-hall, and traditional half-timbering beyond (opposite).

zoo's founder and his animals; Delacour then purchased the château at Clères from the Duchesse de Choiseul-Pralin in 1919. There he started to assemble his collection of rare birds and mammals, plants and trees, many of which he gathered during his travels to distant parts of the world.

The château, extending in a variety of architectural styles from around the original thirteenth-century manor-house, also received his attention; the main reception rooms were transformed into an extremely grand indoor aviary.

Not that the lavishing of such care on his fortunate birds meant that Delacour was a reclusive type without much time for his own species: urbane and popular, he held successive directorships of the aviaries of Los Angeles, New York and Washington, before ending his days in California at the age of 95. Even in his nineties he would still return to the wooded valley of the Clérette to watch his favourite collection pacing and fluttering among the trees that he had planted, and seen grow to maturity.

The countryside for miles around Étretat is dotted with extravagant-looking holiday villas in revivalist styles (left). *The houses of the village itself, though, are compactly arranged between beach and cliffs* (opposite).

Étretat

THE SCENIC BEAUTY of Étretat, sited picturesquely on the Côte d'Albâtre north of Le Havre, has long exerted a magnetic attraction for creative spirits. The earliest painter to spot the potential of its cliff formations was Isabey, whose famous portraits of Napoleon astride his snorting charger assured him a favoured position at the Imperial court. Isabey first visited Étretat in the 1840s, followed by socially privileged tourists. Among these was the retiring Queen of Spain, Isabelle, who took a lease on a splendid château half-way up the cliffs to the east of the village. This property, the Château des Aygues, filled with original furnishings from the period and surrounded by a pretty park, can be visited today.

A casino soon followed, built in 1852, and a stylish new esplanade, in the wake of the fashionable vogue for bathing in the sea. The beach that curves invitingly between the two massive cliffs was perfect for bathers, as it remains today, sheltered from the prevailing wind by the vast bulk of the Falaise d'Amont. Ascending this cliff, energetic holidaymakers can enjoy dramatic views of the Falaise d'Aval at the other end of the beach and dose themselves on an inexhaustible supply of health-giving sea breezes, while golf devotees struggle on the cliff-top links.

Historically, the beach *is* Étretat – there is no record of a fishing settlement here, as there is no natural harbour. But on the heels of the Parisian socialites who flocked here each summer came the artists. These were to include Eugène Delacroix, Eugène Boudin, himself a native of Honfleur, and, later, the most celebrated visitor of them all, Claude Monet. His dozens of canvases of the famous cliff formation make their forms seem almost familiar to the first-time visitor, for all their innate strangeness.

*A*lthough often crowded cheek by jowl, the villas of Étretat manage to
assert their individuality, maybe in the form of a pointed turret
or upturned boat (opposite *and* above left and right). *For a view of the
whole village and its surroundings, there is no better spot than the steps
of the seamen's chapel, Notre-Dame-de-la-Garde (left).*

The lantern tower of Saint-Sulpice rises beyond the market square (right), *but the church's main claim to architectural distinction is its outstandingly beautiful sixteenth-century wooden screen* (opposite).

A MAIN STREET which straightens and broadens after crossing the little river Crevon, modest shop fronts facing each other with an air of prosperous calm: there is nothing about the village of Ry and its quiet valley to suggest calamity or scandal. But in 1854, as is witnessed by a memorial stone in the churchyard, the sensational fate of a local woman must have been the talk of the whole district. Indeed, one imagines that if the propensity for gossip was as strong in rural communities then as now, her ill-starred adventures would have been discussed long before her demise. The object of this public attention was Delphine Couturier, the young and pretty wife of the local doctor. She carried on an affair with a local landowner, slipping out of the side-gate of her garden to hasten to his house, the Manoir de la Huchette. The reason that the unhappy fate of Madame Couturier, who took poison after the discovery of her infidelity, should engage the attention of the visitor to Ry is of course that her story reached the ears of Gustave Flaubert. A frequent visitor to nearby Rouen, he later turned the doctor's wife into the heroine of his celebrated novel, *Madame Bovary*.

Ry

*F*amous as the probable inspiration for the setting of Flaubert's
Madame Bovary, *Ry has many delightful lanes and byways: from the*
Côté des Grellemonts near Saint-Sulpice (opposite); *the presbytery near*
the Rue Dequinnemare (above) *which now houses a religious order.*

*M*any of the village's most attractive spots, including a former watering
place for horses, are to be found near the river Crevon and its tributaries
(above *and* opposite).

*T*he restored Romanesque chapel of the abbey (above) *and its grounds are now home to the Benedictine sisters of Notre-Dame-du-Pré. Secular power is represented by the much expanded château* (opposite), *originally begun in the 12th century.*

Valmont

WHATEVER BECAME of the convent founded by the Countess Lesceline at Saint-Pierre-sur-Dives in 1012, which in 1046 was replaced by a monastery? Such is not a question likely to have taxed any but the most minutely curious visitor to Normandy. Even so, it provided some unexpected satisfaction, at least to the author of this book, to wander up the quiet valley of the river Valmont and stumble across the answer.

The Benedictine sisters, after being driven out of Saint-Pierre by local spite, withdrew to the town of Lisieux, where they began a much longer tenure at their convent of Saint-Désir-de-Lisieux. Nine-hundred-and-forty-five years later, finding it impossible to follow their life of silent contemplation alongside the Rue de Caen, now become the noisome N13, they moved to this quiet valley. Valmont offered them perfect peace, and a beautiful ruined abbey, deserted by its monks since the Revolution. This must have appeared to be an answer to the sisters' prayers, as of course it was. In their new spiritual home they have re-roofed and reconsecrated the Romanesque church, formerly a ruin painted by Delacroix, a frequent visitor to Valmont.

From the far side of the valley, the abbey is overlooked by an equally ancient survival of a different character: the former fortress-home of the mighty Estouteville family. This is a rugged twelfth-century keep, flanked by two later wings, one dating from Louis XI's reign, and the other begun sixty years afterwards in the first flush of the new Renaissance fashion.

Spread between convent and castle, the village of Valmont now goes quietly about its business, no longer famous for the weaving that used to dominate the valley, its grain silo and attendant railway station silent and disused. The place has a quiet, demure charm, attractive no doubt to a sisterhood wandering in the contemporary wilderness.

*E*ngaging details are formed by the pretty village dwellings along the river Valmont and a disused railway line (this page). *It is hard, however, to escape the looming presence of the château* (opposite), *just visible through the trees of the abbey grounds.*

Varengeville-sur-Mer

Villas partly hidden in woodland (opposite) and vistas along the Normandy coastline (here, east towards Pourville) characterize this secluded community.

UNLIKE MANY OTHER resorts along the Côte d'Albâtre, Varengeville manages to hide its charms from the motorist who merely travels through it en route west from nearby Dieppe. Indeed, unless the rather flamboyant Mairie is glimpsed beside the road that winds across the well-wooded promontory, it is easy to miss this community hiding among the trees. But such is the character of Varengeville: its many villas dotted among these woods were designed for seclusion.

Here, the glamorous list of *habitués* begins with the painters Isabey, Corot and Monet in the nineteenth century, followed in the next century by some of the most distinguished figures of modernism, notably Georges Braque, who owned a house there, Kandinsky, Arp and Léger. They enjoyed the quiet seclusion of their discreetly sited villas, undisturbed on their cliff-top by the hordes who flocked to the coast at sea-level, by the day or by the week. Then as now, the summer denizens of Varengeville inclined to measure their vacations by the season.

In August 1942, this cliff-top haven became the location of a very different invasion. Allied commanders on the other side of the Channel chose the stretch of coast west of Dieppe to launch a series of commando raids, designed to test the defences of the occupying German forces. Perhaps because their sector included the lightly guarded cliffs by Varengeville or because, having gained the cliffs, they were able to move inland without detection through the thick woods, the British unit captured its objective, the German headquarters next to the lighthouse at Ailly. Landing on the exposed beaches to the east and west, the Canadian forces were not so fortunate, and suffered terrible losses before withdrawing. The Dieppe raid turned out to be an exploit of huge bravery but questionable utility, although its painful lessons played their part in the planning of the huge invasion two years later.

*A*ltough the opulently appointed private villa
(top) *can often seem to be the most typical type
of residence of Varengeville, more modest, though
undeniably well-kept dwellings do exist (above).
The twelfth-century church of Saint-Valéry (right)
occupies a much more dramatic and exposed site at
the sea's edge*

*T*he house and gardens of Le Bois des Moutiers (above *and* opposite) make an extraordinary ensemble on the Normandy coast, derived as they are from the design principles of the English Arts and Crafts Movement. Edwin Lutyens, then 29, designed the house in 1898, while the gardens were the work of Gertrude Jekyll, creating one of the pair's famously harmonious collaborations.

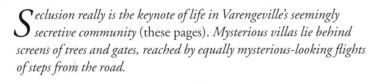

*S*eclusion really is the keynote of life in Varengeville's seemingly
secretive community (these pages). *Mysterious villas lie behind
screens of trees and gates, reached by equally mysterious-looking flights
of steps from the road.*

Villequier

A FEW MILES DOWNSTREAM from Caudebec-en-Caux, which sits at the northernmost point of one of the Seine's most flamboyant loops, the river widens out in front of the small village of Villequier, a gem of a place stretching along the northern bank at the foot of a wooded slope. This has been home to generations of sailors and fishermen, as well as the river pilots who took over here from the estuary pilots bringing ships up from Le Havre. Today, secluded and attractive, it is more likely to be the

home of an oil-company executive from the vast refinery downstream at Port-Jérôme.

The riverside quay provides a particularly pleasant walk; overlooking it is a row of elegant houses, the finest of which now houses a museum devoted to memorabilia of the family of Victor Hugo. The displays there do not show him as a grand old man of French letters, but concentrate on his personal life. He often stayed in the village with his close friend Auguste Vacquerie, son of a wealthy

*F*amous for its association with Victor Hugo, Villequier is a place of exceptional beauty. Pretty brick and half-timbered houses line its main street (left *and* above), *and a promenade runs the whole length of the village along the bank of the river Seine* (opposite).

*T*he houses along the Rue
 Ernest Binet (opposite),
including the Vacquerie house
used by Hugo (above), *have large*
gardens giving on to the river.

shipbuilding family who owned the house. In 1843,
they celebrated the happy wedding of Vacquerie's
brother, Charles, and Hugo's daughter, Léopoldine.
Tragically, the newly-weds were drowned in a
boating accident only six months after they had
been married. This cruel blow, to a man still
regaining his equilibrium after the death of his wife

Adèle, inspired the moving poetry of his famous
Contemplations. The ill-fated couple are buried, with
Adèle, beside the parish church of Saint-Martin.
Inside the church, sixteenth-century stained-glass
windows show a lively naval battle between the ships
of the Dieppe adventurer, Jean Ango, and a fleet of
Portuguese merchantmen.

*T*he old-established Auberge du Vieux Puits at Pont-Audemer (Eure) is notable both for its food and its fine traditional interior (left).

Eating in Normandy

VISITORS TO NORMANDY have always enjoyed emulating the hearty appetites of the local population, which has traditionally produced some of the most sumptuous foodstuffs in French gastronomy. Normandy butter, especially from around Isigny-sur-Mer, is of unparalleled quality and forms the basis for many dishes. In Camembert, Livarot and Neufchâtel respectively are produced the three great cheeses of the region. Each has its own distinctive character and all are world-famous. From the coast comes a wealth of sea food, and no waiter would presume to hurry a diner who has elected to work through one of the gargantuan pyramidal displays of shell-fish that are a common sight in the province, especially in coastal towns and villages.

Apples (and, to the south-west, pears) are another of Normandy's staples. As well as providing the filling for countless delicious tarts and pies, the many apple orchards are mainly devoted to the production of cider and of the famous calvados apple brandy which is distilled from it. This 'calva' is consumed in considerable quantities all over Normandy, but with little of the seriousness and mystique that surrounds its grape equivalent in Cognac. It is not at all unusual to start the working day with a 'café-calva', and it is also slipped into the middle of a traditional Norman feast, in the guise of what is described as 'le trou normand' – a shot of the fiery spirit intended to encourage the digestion of the first half of the meal and to create a new hole in the stomach to make room for the next onslaught. Such dedication to food consumption might seem excessive, but not once the deliciousness of Normandy's cuisine has been experienced at first hand.

*T*wo gastronomic delights of Normandy: Camembert (above) *is one of the three great cheeses of the province; at the* Auberge du Vieux-Puits, *the* panier des pêcheurs *reminds us that much of the cuisine here is dependent on the fruits of the sea.*

A Travellers' Guide

Regional Tourist Office
14 rue Charles-Corbeau, Evreux;
tel. (0232) 337900.
(www.normandy-tourism.org)

Manche

Departmental Tourist Office
Maison du Département, Route de Villedieu,
Saint-Lô; tel. (0233) 059870.

Barfleur

SIGHTS & EVENTS
Market day, Saturdays.
WHERE TO STAY
Hôtel Le Conquérant, 16 rue Thomas Becket;
tel. (0233) 540082.
WHERE TO EAT
Hôtel-Restaurant Le Phare, 42 rue Thomas Becket;
tel. (0233) 541033.
INFORMATION
2 quai Henri Chardon; tel. (0233) 540248.

Mont-Saint-Michel

SIGHTS & EVENTS
Abbey, open all year except 11 January, 1 May, 1 & 11
November and 25 December.
WHERE TO STAY
Hôtel-Restaurant Saint-Pierre; tel. (0233) 601403.
Hôtel-Restaurant La Vieille Auberge;
tel. (0233) 601434.
WHERE TO EAT
Restaurant-Crêperie La Sirène; tel. (0233) 600860.
INFORMATION
Cours de l'Avancée; tel. (0233) 601430.

Mortain

SIGHTS & EVENTS
Market day, Saturdays.
L'Abbaye Blanche, avenue de l'Abbaye Blanche;
tel. (0233) 590021.
WHERE TO STAY
Hôtel-Restaurant de la Poste, 1 place des Arcades;
tel. (0233) 590055.
WHERE TO EAT
See above.
INFORMATION
Rue du Bourg Lopin; tel. (0233) 591974.

Regnéville-sur-Mer

WHERE TO STAY
Hostellerie de la Baie, 4 rue du Port;
tel. (0233) 074394.
WHERE TO EAT
See above.

INFORMATION
Syndicat d'Initiative, 8 rue du Port; tel. (0233)
458871.

Saint-Vaast-la-Hougue

SIGHTS & EVENTS
Ferry crossings to the Île Tatihou from L'Acceuil
Tatihou, quai Vauban, nr. the information office;
tel. (0233) 231992.
WHERE TO STAY
Hôtel-Restaurant de France / Les Fuchsias, 20 rue
Maréchal Foch; tel. (0233) 544226.
Hôtel-Restaurant La Granitière, 74 rue Maréchal
Foch; tel. (0233) 545899.
WHERE TO EAT
Restaurant La Chasse Marée, 8 place du Général de
Gaulle; tel. (0233) 231408.
INFORMATION
1 place du Général de Gaulle; tel. (0233) 544137.

Vauville

SIGHTS & EVENTS
Botanic garden, open in the afternoons; daily in July
& August, only Tuesdays & weekends in May &
September.
WHERE TO STAY
Hôtel-Restaurant de la Poste, 39 rue Jallot,
Beaumont-Hague; tel. (0233) 527145.
WHERE TO EAT
Restaurant La Croix-Frimot, place de Ville, Croix-
Frimot, nr. Biville; tel. (0233) 528390.
INFORMATION
Office du Tourisme de la Hague, 45 rue Jallot,
Beaumont-Hague; tel. (0233) 527494.

Villedieu-les-Poêles

SIGHTS & EVENTS
Leather workshop, open Monday to Saturday all
year, Sundays in July & August only; 54 rue
Général Huard; tel. (0233) 513185.
Bell foundry, open daily in July & August, closed
Sunday, Monday for the rest of the year; rue du
Pont-Chignon; tel. (0233) 610056.
Market day, Tuesdays.
WHERE TO STAY
Hôtel-Restaurant Le Fruitier, place des Costils;
tel. (0233) 905100.
Hôtel-Restaurant Manoir de l'Acherie, 2 km east at
L'Acherie; tel. (0233) 511387.
Hôtel-Restaurant Saint-Pierre et Saint-Michel, place
de la République; tel. (0233) 610011.

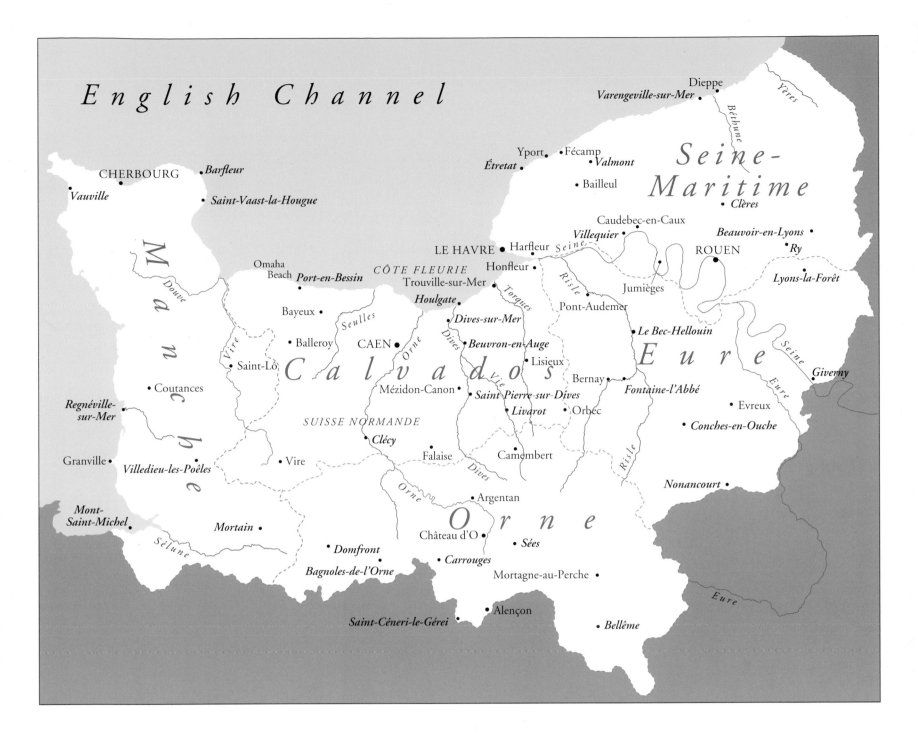

Hôtel-Restaurant Les Visiteurs, 57 rue Général
Huard; tel. (0233) 610113.

WHERE TO EAT
Restaurant Le Conquistador, 46 rue du Bourg
l'Abbesse; tel. (0233) 610617.

INFORMATION
Place des Costils; tel. (0233) 610569.

Calvados

Departmental Tourist Office
Place du Canada, Caen; tel. (0231) 865330.

Beuvron-en-Auge

WHERE TO STAY
Hôtel-Restaurant Auberge de la Boule d'Or, place de
la Village; tel. (0231) 797878.
Le Manoir des Sens (guest house), route de la Forge
de Clermont; tel. (0231) 792305.

WHERE TO EAT
Restaurant Pavé d'Auge, place de la Village;
tel. (0231) 792671.

INFORMATION
Place de la Village; tel. (0231) 390985.

Clécy

WHERE TO STAY
Hôtel-Restaurant Moulin du Vey, by Pont du Vey;
tel. (0231) 697108.
M. Aubry at La Loterie (guest house), rue de la
Loterie; tel. (0231) 697438.

WHERE TO EAT
Restaurant Au Fil de l'Eau, on the banks of the
Orne; tel. (0231) 697113.

INFORMATION
Place du Tripot; tel. (0231) 697995.

*T*he famous trou normand (above): *this shot of calvados, taken after the first course of dinner, prepares the digestive system for the more substantial delights to follow.*

Dives-sur-Mer

SIGHTS & EVENTS
Market day, Saturday mornings.
WHERE TO STAY
Hôtel d'Hastings, 6 rue d'Hastings; tel. (0231) 280200.
Hôtel-Restaurant de la Marine, 75 rue du Port; tel. (0231) 910418.
WHERE TO EAT
Restaurant-Brasserie Le Mora, 89 rue du Port; tel. (0231) 912587.
Restaurant-Brasserie Le Shaker, 13 rue du Général de Gaulle; tel. (0231) 918100.
INFORMATION
9 rue du Général de Gaulle; tel. (0231) 912466.

Houlgate

SIGHTS & EVENTS
Market day, Thursdays.
WHERE TO STAY
Hôtel Auberge des Aulnettes, route de la Corniche; tel. (0231) 280028.
Hôtel du Centre, 31 rue des Bains; tel. (0231) 248040.
Hôtel-Restaurant Le 1900, 17 rue des Bains; tel. (0231) 287777.
Hôtel Saint-Cecilia, 25 rue des Alliés; tel. (0231) 287171.
WHERE TO EAT
Restaurant Maison des Coquillages, 37 rue des Bains; tel.(0231) 248217.
INFORMATION
10 boulevard des Belges; tel. (0231) 243479.

Livarot

SIGHTS & EVENTS
Cheese museum, open April to October, Manoir de l'Isle, rue Marcel Gambier; tel. (0231) 634313.
Market day, Sunday mornings.
WHERE TO STAY
Hôtel-Restaurant Le Vivier, place de la Mairie; tel. (0231) 320410.
WHERE TO EAT
Restaurant-Crêperie La Sarrazine, 28 rue Marcel Gambier; tel. (0231) 635048.
INFORMATION
Place Georges Bisson; tel. (0231) 634739.

Port-en-Bessin

SIGHTS & EVENTS
Market day, Sunday mornings.
WHERE TO STAY
Hôtel-Restaurant La Chenevière, 1.5 km south, at Escure-Commes; tel. (0231) 512525.
WHERE TO EAT
Restaurant Le Vent d'Amont, 39 rue Nationale; tel. (0231) 920592.
INFORMATION
2 rue du Croiseur-Montcalm; tel. (0231) 219233.

Saint-Pierre-sur-Dives

SIGHTS & EVENTS
Abbey and gardens; apply at tourist office for individual/group visits; opening times vary.
Market day, Mondays.
WHERE TO STAY
Hôtel-Restaurant Les Agriculteurs, 118 rue de la Falaise; tel. (0231) 207278.
Hôtel-Restaurant La France, 11 place du Marché; tel. (0231) 207466.
WHERE TO EAT
Restaurant-Crêperie Le Balladin, 134 rue de la Falaise; tel. (0231) 203963.
INFORMATION
23 rue Saint-Benoist; tel. (0231) 209790.

Orne

Departmental Tourist Office:
88 rue de Saint-Blaise, Alençon; tel. (0233) 288871.

Bagnoles-de-l'Orne

SIGHTS & EVENTS
Thermal baths, open April to October, rue Professeur Louvel; tel. (0233) 303800.
Market day, Saturdays.
WHERE TO STAY
Hôtel-Restaurant Le Bois-Joli, 12 avenue Philippe du Rozier; tel. (0233) 379277.
Hôtel-Restaurant La Potinière du Lac, rue des Casinos; tel. (0233) 306500.
Hôtel-Restaurant Le Roc au Chien, rue Professeur Louvel; tel. (0233) 379733.
Hôtel-Restaurant Le Pavillon du Moulin, rue Professeur Louvel; tel. (0233) 378343.
Hôtel-Restaurant La Terrasse, place de la République; tel. (0233) 306363.
WHERE TO EAT
See above.
INFORMATION
Place du Marché; tel. (0233) 378566.

Bellême

SIGHTS & EVENTS
Market day, Thursday mornings.
WHERE TO STAY
Hôtel-Restaurant Du Golf, Les Sablons, route du Mans; tel. (0233) 851313.
Hôtel-Restaurant Relais Saint-Louis, 1 boulevard Bansard-des-Bois; tel. (0233) 731211.
WHERE TO EAT
Restaurant L'Auberge des Trois Juges, 8 km east, at Nocé; tel. (0233) 734103.
Restaurant La Boule d'Or, place du Général Leclerc; tel. (0233) 259932.
INFORMATION
Boulevard Bansard-des-Bois; tel. (0233) 730969.

Carrouges

SIGHTS & EVENTS
Château, open daily except 1 January, 1 May, 1 & 11 November and 25 December.
WHERE TO STAY
Hôtel-Restaurant du Nord, place du Général de Gaulle; tel. (0233) 272014.
Hôtel-Restaurant Saint-Pierre, place du Général de

Gaulle; tel. (0233) 272002.

WHERE TO EAT
Restaurant Au Lignière, rue du Chapitre; tel. (0233) 272012.

INFORMATION
24 place du Général le Veneur; tel. (0233) 274062.

Domfront

SIGHTS & EVENTS
Market day, Saturdays.

WHERE TO STAY
Hôtel-Restaurant de France, 7 rue du Mont-Saint-Michel; tel. (0233) 385144.
Hôtel-Restaurant Le Relais Saint-Michel, 5 rue du Mont-Saint-Michel; tel. (0233) 386499.
M. & Mme. Tailhandier-Jacobson (guest house), 1 rue de Godras; tel. (0233) 371003.

WHERE TO EAT
Restaurant L'Auberge Grandgousier, 1 place de la Liberté; tel. (0233) 389717.

INFORMATION
12 place de la Roirie; tel. (0233) 385397.

Saint-Céneri-le-Gérei

SIGHTS & EVENTS
Painters' festival, every year over the Easter weekend.

WHERE TO STAY
Hôtel La Giroise, Le Bourg; tel. (0233) 267167.

WHERE TO EAT
Restaurant Auberge des Peintres, Le Bourg; tel. (0233) 264918.
Restaurant-Crêperie La Maréchalerie, route de Saint-Pierre; tel. (0233) 820171.

INFORMATION
At Fresnay-sur-Sarthe, 19 avenue du Docteur Riant; tel. (0243) 332804.

Sées

SIGHTS & EVENTS
Market day, Saturday mornings.

WHERE TO STAY
Hôtel-Restaurant Le Cheval Blanc, place Saint-Pierre; tel. (0233) 278048.
Hôtel-Restaurant Le Dauphin, 31 place des Halles; tel. (0233) 278007.
Hôtel-Restaurant L'Isle de Sées, 5 km north-west, at Macé; tel. (0233) 279865.
Hôtel-Restaurant Le Saint-Louis, 9 rue Billy; tel. (0233) 278943.

WHERE TO EAT
Restaurant Le Gourmand Candide, place de la Cathédrale; tel. (0233) 279128.
Restaurant Le Relais des Cordeliers, 5 enclos des Cordeliers; tel. (0233) 271995.

INFORMATION
Place du Général de Gaulle; tel. (0233) 287479.

Eure

Departmental Tourist Office:
Boulevard George-Chauvin, Evreux; tel. (0232) 315151.

Conches-en-Ouche

SIGHTS & EVENTS
Market day, Thursdays.

WHERE TO STAY
Hôtel-Restaurant Le Cygne, 2 rue Paul Guilbaud;

*A*s the basic ingredient of both food and drink in the province (left *and* above), *the apple is central to Norman gastronomy.*

*N*othing could be more typical of farming in the Eure *département than this still and storage barrels* (above *and* below right) *at a cider farm.*

tel. (0232) 302060.
Hôtel-Restaurant La Grand' Mare, 13 avenue Croix de Fer; tel. (0232) 302330.
WHERE TO EAT
Restaurant La Toque Blanche, 18 place Carnot; tel. (0232) 300154.
INFORMATION
Place Aristide-Briand; tel. (0232) 307642.

Fontaine-l'Abbé

WHERE TO STAY
Hôtel Le Lion d'Or, 48 rue du Général de Gaulle, Bernay; tel. (0232) 431206.
M. Gouffier & M. Rodriguez at *Domaine de Plessis* (guest house), 5 km south-west, at Saint-Clair d'Arcey; tel. (0232) 466000.
M. & Mme. Parent at *Manoir du Val* (guest house), 6 km south, at Saint-Aubin-le-Guichard; tel. (0232) 444104.
INFORMATION
At Bernay, 29 rue Thiers; tel. (0232) 433208.

Giverny

SIGHTS & EVENTS
Maison Claude Monet, open April to October 10.00–18.00, closed Mondays.
WHERE TO STAY
Les Agapanthes (guest house), 65 rue Claude Monet; tel. (0232) 210159.
WHERE TO EAT
Restaurant Ancien Hôtel Baudy, 81 rue Claude Monet; tel. (0232) 211003.
Restaurant Les Jardins de Giverny (closed evenings); tel. (0232) 216086.
Restaurant La Terrasse, 87 rue Claude Monet; tel. (0232) 513609.
INFORMATION
35 rue Carnot, Vernon; tel. (0232) 513960.

Le Bec-Hellouin

SIGHTS & EVENTS
Abbaye Notre-Dame, guided tours daily except Saturdays.
WHERE TO STAY
Hôtel-Restaurant L'Auberge de l'Abbaye, place Guillaume le Conquérant; tel. (0232) 448602.
Mme. Caron at *Le Bec-Hellouin* (guest house), place Guillaume le Conquérant; tel. (0232) 461936.
WHERE TO EAT
Restaurant Crêperie du Bec, place de l'Abbé Herluin; tel. (0232) 457905.

Lyons-la-Forêt

SIGHTS & EVENTS
Market day, Thursday & Saturday mornings.
WHERE TO STAY
Hôtel-Restaurant Domaine Saint-Paul, at northern edge of village; tel. (0232) 596057.
Hôtel-Restaurant La Licorne, 27 place Isaac de Bensérade; tel. (0232) 496202.
Hôtel-Restaurant Le Relais de la Lieure, 10 km south-west, at Menesqueville; tel. (0232) 490621.
Mme. Nitschmann at *Château de Rosay* (guest house), 5 km south-west, route de Lyons, Rosay-sur-Lieure; tel. (0232) 496651.
WHERE TO EAT
Restaurant de la Halle, 6 place Isaac de Bensérade; tel. (0232) 494992.
INFORMATION
20 rue de l'Hôtel de Ville; tel. (0232) 493165.

Nonancourt

SIGHTS & EVENTS
Market day, Wednesday mornings.
WHERE TO STAY
Hôtel Le Beffroi, 12 place Métézeau, 12 km east, at Dreux; tel. (0237) 500203.
M. & Mme. Demory at *La Rançonnière* (guest house), 3 km east, at Saint-Germain-sur-Avre; tel. (0232) 601010.

WHERE TO EAT

Restaurant L'Auberge de la Vallée Verte, 13 km east, at Vernouillet; tel. (0237) 460404.
Restaurant La Flambée, 22 place Aristide-Briand; tel. (0232) 600968.
Restaurant Saint-Pierre, 19 rue Sénarmont, 12 km east, at Dreux; tel. (0237) 464700.

INFORMATION

4 rue Porte-Chartraine, at Dreux; tel. (0237) 460173.

Seine-Maritime

Departmental Tourist Office:

6 rue Couronné, Bihorel-lès-Rouen; tel. (0235) 592626.

Beauvoir-en-Lyons

WHERE TO STAY

Hôtel-Restaurant Auberge des Pilotis, place du Marché; tel. (0235) 907100.

INFORMATION

9 place d'Armes, Gournay-en-Bray; tel. (0235) 902834.

Clères

SIGHTS & EVENTS

Parc zoologique, open daily mid-March to end November.
Market day, Friday afternoons.

WHERE TO STAY

Hôtel-Restaurant au Souper Fin, 4 km north-east, at Frichemesnil; tel. (0235) 333388.
M. & Mme. Degosne (guest house), at Le Tôt, 1 km south-west, route de Montville; tel. (0235) 333438.
M. & Mme. Molière at *Les Marettes* (guest house), 2 km south-west, route de Montville; tel. (0235) 334784.

WHERE TO EAT

Restaurant Auberge du Moulin, at Le Tôt, 1 km south-west, route de Montville.

INFORMATION

59 avenue du Parc; tel. (0235) 333864.

T he twin themes of the Normandy countryside, cattle and cider orchards, are captured here in late autumn tranquillity.

Étretat

SIGHTS & EVENTS
Market day, Thursdays.
WHERE TO STAY
Hôtel des Falaises, 1 boulevard René Coty; tel. (0235) 270277.
Hôtel-Restaurant Dormy House, route du Havre; tel. (0235) 270788.
M. Benicourt (guest house), 24 avenue de Verdun; tel. (0235) 100565.
WHERE TO EAT
Restaurant Le Galion, boulevard René Coty; tel. (0235) 294874.
INFORMATION
Place Maurice Guillard; tel. (0235) 270521.

Ry

SIGHTS & EVENTS
Market day, Saturdays.
WHERE TO STAY
M. & Mme. Cousin (guest house), at Auzouville-sur-Ry, 5 km south-west; tel. (0235) 234074.
WHERE TO EAT
Restaurant-Rôtisserie Bovary, Grande Rue, next to the Mairie; tel. (0235) 236146.
INFORMATION
Maison de l'Abreuvoir, Grande Rue; tel. (0235) 231990.

Valmont

WHERE TO STAY
Hôtel Château de Sassetot-le-Mauconduit, 7 km north, at Sassetot-le-Mauconduit; tel. (0235) 280011.
Mme. Cachera (guest house), La Clos du Vivier, 4/6 chemin du Vivier; tel. (0235) 299095.
WHERE TO EAT
Restaurant d'Agriculture, 9 rue d'Estoutville; tel. (0235) 298425.

Restaurant-Auberge Le Bec au Cauchois, 22 route de Fécamp; tel. (0235) 297756.
INFORMATION
Place du Docteur Dupont; tel. (0235) 100812.

Varengeville-sur-Mer

SIGHTS & EVENTS
Manoir d'Ango, open mid-March to mid-November, route de Tous-les-Mesnils; tel. (0235) 851480.
Le Parc des Moutiers, garden open mid-March to mid-November, rue de l'Église; tel. (0235) 851002.
WHERE TO STAY
Hôtel-Restaurant de la Terrasse, route de Vasterival; tel. (0235) 851254.
Mme. Poggiale at *La Thébaïde* (guest house), 577 rue des Verts Bois, Pourville; tel. (0235) 842114.
WHERE TO EAT
Restaurant Le Trou Normand, rue des Verts Bois, Pourville; tel. (0235) 845984.
INFORMATION
Rue des Verts Bois, at Pourville; tel. (0235) 847106.

Villequier

SIGHTS & EVENTS
Victor Hugo Museum, open all year, closed Tuesdays & Sunday mornings, rue Ernest Binet; tel. (0235) 567831.
WHERE TO STAY
Hôtel-Restaurant Le Grand Sapin; tel. (0235) 567873.
Pub with rooms, *The Coach House Inn*, on the banks of the Seine; tel. (0235) 567870.
INFORMATION
Place du Général de Gaulle, at Caudebec-en-Caux; tel. (0232) 704632.

Further reading

BEHAGE, Dominique, *Gastronomie Normande,* Colmar, 1986

BENTLEY, James, *Normandy,* London, 1989

BONNETON, Christine (ed.), *Normandie – Écologie, Économie, Art, Littérature, Histoire, Traditions Populaires, Condé-sur-Noireau,* 1978

BRIER, Max-André & BRUNER, Pierre, *L'Architecture Rurale Française,* Paris, 1984

BROWN, R. ALLEN, *The Normans,* London, 1974

COURSIER, Alain, *Normandie,* Paris, 1981

DAVIS, R.H.C., *Normans and their Myths,* London, 1976

GUIDES GALLIMARD, *Manche, Eure & Calvados,* Paris, 1996–98

HUNT, Robert & MASSON, David, *The Normandy Campaign,* London, 1976

KEEGAN, John, *Six Armies in Normandy,* London, 1992

KLEIN, Jacques-Sylvain, *Normandie, Berceau d'Impressionisme,* Rennes, 1999

LEPROHON, Pierre & MARINIE, Arlette, *La Normandie,* Geneva, 1982

MABIRE, Jean et al., *Histoire Secrète de la Normandie,* Paris, 1984

McNEILL, John, *The Blue Guide to Normandy,* London, 1993